the

HAPPY EVERYTHING
COOKBOOK

by Coton Colors

the HAPPY EVERYTHING COOKBOOK

by Coton Colors

Start with one clever DESIGNER;
Add a curious COOK;
Mix in irresistible recipes;
Season with a dash of storytelling;
Pair with a BIG glass of wine &
Be prepared to feast on something...

FABULOUS!

LAURA JOHNSON & SUSAN MURRAY
- clever designer -   - curious cook -

The Happy Everything Cookbook

Inquiries or requests to the Publisher for permission should be
addressed to:

P2P Publishing
3365 Garber Drive
Tallahassee, FL 32303
(850) 383-1111
www.p2pPublish.com

For ordering information or information on any Coton Colors
products, please contact our Customer Service Department:
(877) 801-1292
www.Coton-Colors.com

Produced by Coton Colors Inc.
Photographs © 2011 Linley Paske
Recipes © 2011 Susan Murray
(except for those credited within this book)

The Happy Everything Collection © by Coton Colors Express, LLC.
All other products referenced in the book are trademarks of their
respective companies.

Printed in the United States
ISBN 978-0-615-49083-0

First Printing {October 2011}

Tasty ideas to
stir new traditions
& create happy
memories.

Happy Everything!

The INSPIRaTION
behind the cookbook...

I've always loved celebrating, from the predictable, familiar family birthdays to the spontaneity of last minute, impromptu gatherings. Through Coton Colors, I've had the distinct joy of growing a business marrying my passions of handcrafted artistry with inspiration for celebratory moments. We joyously create hand-painted pottery designed to exemplify chic sophistication, with a touch of fun... exuding the creativity with which I live my own life.

The Happy Everything platter is my favorite creation, and the collection grew out of my innate desire to attach a little bit of "happy" to everything. To me, living life in style means finding smiles in the most ordinary of moments. After years of considering capturing these concepts in a cookbook, I finally gathered the most important ingredient necessary - my talented friend, Susan "Susie" Murray - to share her recipes and her seasoned entertaining philosophies. An invite to Susie's home for dinner is a true treasure... I never pass up the opportunity to experience her delicious and detailed menus.

Like many others, young married life and early parenthood found both Susie and I making the mistake of working entirely too hard to impress. We were chronic over-achievers and the desire to have everything "done right" was paralyzing at times. Were our homes perfectly presentable? Were the flowers precisely placed? Was the food hot and ready as guests arrived? And moreover, was it delicious enough to wow? Were our children on their best behavior {or could we quickly get them fed and to bed}? Fortunately, it didn't take us long to realize... the simple act of hosting friends and family at your table is enough to evoke gratitude from all present. When you look back on your life one day, all that matters is that you enjoyed every day, whether your home was perfect or not!

Years of experience have shaped Susie and I into comfortable entertainers, and "The Happy Everything Cookbook" offers recipes and menus to relish with friends and family, sans the stress and stuffiness. Entertaining – and really life itself – doesn't have to be about over-achieving. The sections in this book are centered around some of our most favorite, happy gatherings. Susie has developed cohesive menus that are complimentary when prepared together, however, we hope you'll be curious and enjoy the individual recipes along with your family favorites as well. The fabulous food, tips and tidbits sprinkled throughout "The Happy Everything Cookbook" are designed to infuse a little "happy" into everything. But the cookbook is about more than tasty recipes and decorating tips – we hope that it sets the tone to truly celebrate the relationships in your life and inspires you to create memorable events you, your family and friends will enjoy for years to come. Make time to celebrate all of the little things... in our eyes, the little things are the big things, after all.

Here's to finding a little happy...
in Everything!

Meet the ClEVER Designer...

Raised in the beauty of Miami, Florida, by a motivated mom and business-minded father, Laura Johnson, founder and owner of Coton Colors, Inc., was entrenched in the colorful culture of Old Florida. Laura's parents' easy entertaining style influenced her love for celebratory occasions from an early age. Surrounded by warm breezes and palm trees, much of her childhood was spent outdoors around the pool or on the beach. Fresh citrus and Florida lobster were staples on the menu... in fact, her brother would frequently thaw out a lobster tail for an after-school snack. Laura's culinary style was influenced by many members of her family - the simplicity of the classic Florida favorites her mom prepared, the delicious dishes her grandmother created and later in life, the Cajun flavors her mother-in-law shared.

Watching her mom sell handmade creations at a few local art fairs ingrained an entrepreneurial spirit in Laura, while her own early talents led to a number of high-level art courses and eventually guided her to Florida State University for a Studio Art degree.

With a constant call to create, the artist can't recall a time in her young adulthood when she wasn't crafting artwork. From the hand-painted cotton clothing that inspired the company's name to the painted ceramics for which she is known today, Laura's keen business sense and artistic motivation has positioned Coton Colors as a leader in the gift industry, encouraging customers to mark all of the celebrations of life with style.

Influenced not only by her childhood in Miami, but also by the Southern charm of Tallahassee where she calls home today, Laura is noted for her impromptu celebrations of ordinary moments. Gatherings with family and friends always gravitate to the kitchen, with Laura revelling in the moment of preparing good food for good company. She brings a creative energy to all endeavors, at home - with her husband, Milton and three daughters Kyle, Sara Kate and Mary Parker - and always to the Coton Colors design center, inspiring her team and her customers alike to live life in style. With her handcrafted designs featured throughout, Laura puts her painting palette down {briefly} to explore the culinary palate, sharing the secrets of her inspired life in "The Happy Everything Cookbook" and providing the ingredients for making every day exceptional.

About Coton Colors

Founded by Laura in 1995, Coton Colors produces collectible home, dining and decorative pieces designed to live life in style. The handcrafted pottery featuring unique and personalized designs creates inspiration fit for every occasion. From its inception, Coton Colors relied on Laura's family ties to make it a successful endeavor. These ties remain today with her father, mother, sister and now daughters working beside her, flourishing as a true family business. Coton Colors products are sought by discerning decorators and original gift seekers across the nation, with the top-selling Happy Everything collection considered a "must-have" for making ordinary moments extraordinary. Coton Colors is available in more than 3,000 stores, encouraging customers to mark all the celebrations of life with chic sophistication and a touch of fun.

Growing up in Central Florida amongst orange groves and a rare peach orchard, a love of fresh Florida produce was imprinted on Susan "Susie" Murray from birth. Susie's best childhood memories involve countless family gatherings spent around Florida-influenced fare. Susie learned from her parents how sharing good food with family and friends can truly be an act of great love.

Once arriving in Tallahassee for college, Susie's sense of fun fashion and her fun-loving personality instantly connected with Laura's creativity. The two became fast friends on the Florida State University campus in the early 80s, later married best friends, raised children together...thus setting the stage for a lifetime of parties and spontaneous get-togethers. Susie and her husband, Ed, like to share their enthusiasm for visiting new places and adventurous eating with their teenagers, Slaton and Kate. Their "eventful" travel and food experiences are often reflected in their dinner parties after they return from a trip.

Susie's unique entertaining philosophy is to bring guests into the kitchen to prepare meals alongside one another, wine or cocktail glass in-hand. She happily sets the stage – getting the house cleaned up, relishing in the planning and shopping for the menu and simply prepping the ingredients beforehand.

With the exception of dessert, the food is not cooked prior to the first guest's arrival. Party guests always help in the food preparation and the entire event becomes interactive, with long evenings spent in the kitchen {isn't this where the best parties happen?}, laughing and learning. The menus can be grandiose – because there are countless hands to help – and in turn, guests gain culinary knowledge and experience a fabulous meal they helped prepare. Through the years, Susie has taught countless friends how to be much more adventurous and confident in the kitchen.

Susie is known for her experimental talent over the stove, with a lifetime of experiences and travel inspiring her to bring friends along on each culinary adventure. Her recipes featured in these pages - along with her insight and cooking tips shared {in her own voice} in each recipe header - are favorites among family and friends and will quickly become yours too.

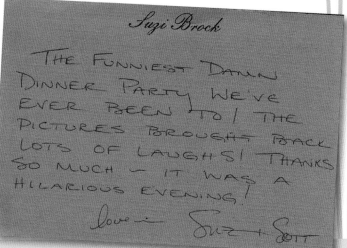

Suzi Brock

THE FUNNIEST DAMN DINNER PARTY WE'VE EVER BEEN TO! THE PICTURES BROUGHT BACK LOTS OF LAUGHS! THANKS SO MUCH — IT WAS A HILARIOUS EVENING!

love — Suzi + Scott

A sweet note to Susie from her friends, Suzi and Scott Brock. Thank you notes are often received after Susie's memorable {and fun!} dinner parties.

Cooking Under Pressure?

Susie was feeling a bit stressed as our team worked on the Cookbook in a frenzied flurry, business as usual to us. We burst out laughing when Susie loudly announced, "I have it all figured out, Laura! You are like a pressure cooker - you thrive under high pressure and you love everyone 'locked' in the pot with you. Me, I'm like a crock-pot - content on simmer - slow and steadily cooking along." This description of these two friends could not be any more accurate. Thank you, Susie, for stepping out of your comfort zone and jumping into the "pressure cooker" with us at Coton Colors!

We are fortune-ate to have you as friends

Contents

Summer Birthday Bar·B·Que

A casual celebration featuring classic fare with a twist

A casual celebration...

I think family birthdays should be celebrated in the simplest of style. Too often, we find ourselves overcome with the magnitude of marking these occasions with proper extravagance, and we lose sight of the real reason for merriment somewhere in the planning and preparation. The simple fact is: easy-to-prepare classic fare and everyone gathered under the same roof are the only ingredients necessary for a memorable party.

My Mom, Dee, will be the first to tell you that she has been highly influential in each of her children's and grand-children's lives, and I wholeheartedly agree. Though her annual summer birthday celebration has always been a happy occasion complete with a full helping of laughter, we've never spent time creating over-the-top themes, difficult décor or multi-course meals. Instead, we leave the stress of preparation behind and truly just enjoy the moment. Since my early days in Miami, my Mom's birthday parties have most often been held on Sunday afternoons, with a tasty yet simple poolside Bar-B-Que. Adults enjoyed fabulous food and company while the kids exhausted themselves with ongoing diving competitions and countless games of Rag Tag in the pool. With my parents now living here in Tallahassee, our family events marking Mom's birthday continue to possess the same casual ambiance... with her granddaughters helping in the cooking and preparation to make the annual event more relaxing for all.

My first taste of the recipes shared in this section immediately brought back memories of being wrapped in a soaking wet towel as we sang "Happy Birthday" to Mom. These recipes are simple classics designed to please the taste buds of even your most critical fans. Susie always says, "Family can be your toughest culinary critics. Keep tried and true recipes in your arsenal for family dinners like birthday Bar-B-Ques. Save and test new recipes when cooking with friends that share your interest in experimenting." It is safe to say when cooking for family, serve well-loved favorites, and your entire crowd will be pleased.

Gifts of a Clever Design

My creative soul strives to find the perfect, out of the ordinary gift for Mom... something to express my gratitude for all she has given our family and a gift that is better than what my siblings will select {just a little friendly competition}. And - a trait of my artistic personality - I tend to wait until the last minute for the inspiration to hit. Over the years this combination has led to countless unique gifts:

- Three tiny chicks that Mom raised in the unlikely suburbs of Miami. These little birds grew into handsome chickens that were very affectionate and interested in her yard work, clucking underfoot as she did her gardening. The best part was the entertaining way they would come running whenever she'd call their names.

- A small kumquat tree that grew to produce an abundance of fruit, which attracted flocks and flocks of wild parrots each year... what a sight!

- A large terracotta bird feeder - she carried it on the airplane home and strapped it in the empty seat next to her... long before the stringent airline codes and carry-on restrictions!

- Hand created gifts reflecting my artistry far too numerous to count - platters fired in school kilns, stitching projects and handmade scrapbook albums created in 3D with mixed media to chronicle a recent vacation... all typically started AND finished the night before Mom's birthday!

A little note from Susie...

Laura is a thoughtful gift giver and most generous by nature. On one occasion, jokingly, I was trying to talk a mutual friend of ours out of her grandmother's aluminum cake carrier. This friend is known to just up and give you something if you covet it, so it is a running joke between the three of us. Sneaky Laura shopped for a similar one online and it arrived at my home just a few days later. Ironically, the carrier still had a piece of masking tape affixed to the bottom placed by the previous owner {as if to identify it at a Sunday supper at church}. The name written was P. Ziegler... my great grandmother's maiden name! Unbelievable! This is the same great grandmother whose chocolate cake recipe we share in this chapter. Though Laura didn't know just how meaningful the gift would prove to be, the unexpected and thoughtful nature with which she selected it was priceless.

Pictured below is the original Coton Colors team... my Mom, Dad, sister, Marcie and brother, Jay! In the early days, each played a large role in getting the company off the ground, be it loading kilns, cleaning pottery, handling finances, setting up our stores and - most importantly, selling our designs. Without them, I would not have gone far! I am so glad that each of us continue to work closely as a team... with more defined roles, I might add! Now the next generation is stepping in...

A Mother's Gifts

"The future destiny of the child is always the work of the mother." — *Napoleon Bonaparte*

Mom celebrating her birthday, 1969

Without intention, Mom's confidence and enthusiasm demands respect and her decisive, to-the-point banter is often experienced by all of us. With an opinion that is almost unfailingly right {she will be the first to say she is NEVER wrong}, she has a power of persuasion like no other. It was Mom's persuasive influences and her eye for my creativity that spawned my artistry and gave birth to the idea of Coton Colors... and while she has given me countless material gifts, her dynamic energy in shaping my future was the best gift of all. She recognized my eye for color and design early on while shuttling me to Wednesday afternoon drawing classes at Mrs. Lovell's home and encouraged my love for ceramics by convincing the Miami Ceramic League to allow a child into their adults-only group.... after one class, they quickly realized I was serious enough about my art to fit in!

Mom noticed the influences on me of the art deco Miami lifestyle and the vibrant Old Florida colors. She was the first to pick up on the fact I often favored more difficult tasks versus simpler methods. This "above and beyond" mantra has progressed through the growth of Coton Colors, challenging us to constantly create products to be better and more impressive than the last. Even today, she is the perfect sounding board for our team, offering well-educated, much-needed direction as we strive to design products that sell well within the retail setting. Visitors to our Tallahassee flagship store also seek her firm advice when selecting their purchases.

Above all, Mom always was and is a "yes" person... she will give me her honest opinion {even if the truth hurts} but she sees beyond the dreams I envision and forges ahead with a "sure we can do it" attitude. It is the present of her constant presence that is my favorite - and the reason for Coton Colors' existence.

-Laura

Mom has always loved her Scotties, 1940

Dynamo Dee...
in the Girls' Words

With my sister and I each having three girls, our family has an abundance of female opinion, and Dee's strong personality has had a profound impact on each granddaughter. I love seeing their distinct personalities in sharing the things they love the most about DeeDee...

DeeDee taught me my love for Scottish Terriers! After we got her a Scottie for her birthday, I fell in love. The next Christmas, Santa brought me my very own Scottie dog, which was by far my favorite gift! DeeDee's cooking is delicious. She finally taught me how to make her famous meatballs. I continue to try to make them, but they are never as good as hers.   *–Logan*

She's always up for teaching you something new {I owe my needle-pointing, cooking, and quilting skills to her.} She's competitive, so playing games with her is always fun - I literally laugh 'til I cry! She doesn't let you live anything down, but in a good way, because it humbles you.   *–Kyle*

DeeDee is ALWAYS there for her family. And... she is also a really good boss!   *–Mary Parker*

DeeDee has a really funny/prankster side. One day when were visiting from Tampa, she pulled me aside to play a prank on the family. That night after our cookout was finished, everyone was sitting around, relaxing. They were talking away, absorbed in the conversation. DeeDee and I slyly snuck away, dressed in dark clothes and painted our faces white. We snuck out on the porch and spooked everyone through the windows. Everyone was screaming and terrified. This was such a fun thing to do with my grandmother and something that I will never forget.   *–Courtney*

I will always remember our days cooking together, drinking hot tea and eating cinnamon toast before nestling into our pallet with all of my cousins on the floor. One of my fondest memories was when she helped me move into my college dorm. This usually is a task that my mom would do but she was in China on dorm move-in day, so DeeDee graciously offered to help. And boy did she! Before long, the entire floor knew her, and she was sharing her opinion with everyone. She was sure to offer her decorating services to anyone that needed them!   *–Taylor*

She gives really good presents. She stands up for what she believes in.   *–Sara Kate*

menu

Grilled Sausage with Arugula

Beer Bread

Tomato Cucumber Salad

Southern Potato Salad

Skillet Baked Beans

BBQ Chicken

Big Milt's Basic BBQ Sauce

Chocolate Chocolate Cake

Grilled Sausage with Arugula

Serves 8

Milton loves to serve sausages as an appetizer, and Laura says he would cook them every night if he had his way. Milton usually serves them grilled, with sweet & spicy honey mustard, but Laura likes to sprinkle them with arugula, feta, and a splash of balsamic vinegar. They always use Bradley's fresh sausage, a Tallahassee favorite. –Susie

8	fresh sausage links
1 bunch	fresh arugula, washed & stems removed
1	(8 ounce) package feta or goat cheese crumbles
	Splash of balsamic vinegar

Prepare and light the grill.

Poke a few holes in each sausage so that they won't burst when grilling. Grill sausages on medium-high heat for 12-15 minutes or until thoroughly cooked.

Remove cooked sausages from the grill and allow them to cool a minute or two before cutting them into bite-size pieces. Place sausage pieces on platter or in bowl.

Sprinkle with arugula, feta, and a splash of balsamic vinegar. Use fingers or toothpicks to eat!

A Little Less Gourmet

Appetizers don't have to be fussy or super sophisticated. In fact, you may find that recipes like these sliced sausages will quickly become friends' favorites. We chuckle at Susie's husband, Ed - who adores great food - yet, he always enjoys the very "non-gourmet" appetizer favorites: Pigs-In-A-Blanket and Cheetos, which our friend serves {in her "tongue-in-cheek" style} just for him prior to her delicious dinners!

Beer Bread

Serves 8, Yields 1 loaf

My grandmother and her sister, Mary, loved to make and eat this bread. The only problem, she was a tee-totaler. We still joke about her having to go down to the store and pull a "hey mister", asking someone to buy her a beer. Laura's mom, Dee, and I were talking about our grandmothers and she said "and I bet her favorite pie was {liquor rich} mince meat... I see a pattern here Susie." We laughed; once again, Dee is always right! –Susie

3 cups	self-rising flour
¼ cup	sugar
	Pinch of salt
1	(12 ounce) beer, room temperature
2 tablespoons	butter, melted

Grease a 9 x 5 x 3 inch loaf pan and set aside.

In a medium bowl, mix flour, sugar, and salt. Stir (room temperature) beer into dry ingredients just until combined. *Do not over mix.*

Pour batter into loaf pan and brush the top with melted butter. Cover with dish towel and allow bread to rise at room temperature for 30 minutes.

Preheat oven to 350 degrees and adjust oven rack to middle position.

Bake for 1 hour until golden. Allow bread to cool a few minutes before slicing. Beer Bread is best served warm and spread with softened butter.

Once cooled, the loaf of beer bread can be kept wrapped in foil. To reheat, slightly open foil so bread doesn't steam and place in oven at 350 degrees until warm. Also, leftovers {if you have any} are good toasted or grilled with a slather of soft butter.

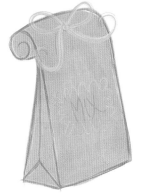

Looking for an Easy Party Favor?

Send your guests home with a little "happy". Beer Bread dry mix makes the perfect gift. Simply mix the dry ingredients and package in little Kraft bags. Create a custom label or hand write the baking instructions on the bag. Attach a recipe card and *voila!*... a thoughtful favor that can be simply mixed with a bottle of beer and baked for a tasty treat long after the party ends.

Tomato Land

When I head out to shop for ingredients for a dinner party, my first stop is always Tomato Land, a produce stand located in Midtown Tallahassee. I enjoy carefully choosing each piece of produce {not pre-packaged} and their selection and prices are always far better than the grocery. Recently, Tomato Land expanded to offer wonderful take-away food, artisan breads and gourmet cheeses and they are the in-town source for locally produced honey and pecans. This is one of my favorite shopping stops, and I believe their farm fresh produce simply tastes better. The fresher the ingredients, the better the meal.   –Susie

Tomato Cucumber Salad
Serves 8-10

While living in Miami, Laura told me there was hardly ever a Sunday when she didn't eat Tomato and Cucumber Salad. Without fail, her dad, Bud, would ask what they were having for dinner and as soon as this salad was mentioned, his eyes would light up. It is truly one of his favorites. Poolside, they would eat this with grilled chicken and baked beans. This refreshing salad is especially good during the summer months when tomatoes are ripe and at their peak.   –Susie

1 pound	assorted tomatoes
¼ teaspoon	salt
1 tablespoon	basil or parsley, chopped
2	large cucumbers, peeled
1	large sweet onion, thinly sliced
1	large green pepper, diced (optional)
2 tablespoons	olive oil
½ cup	white wine vineagar
1 tablespoon	sugar
¼ teaspoon	salt
¼ teaspoon	fine black pepper

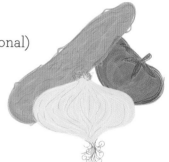

Cut large tomatoes into wedges; if using cherry tomatoes, cut them in half. Lightly salt and sprinkle tomatoes with chopped herbs. Place seasoned tomatoes in a medium bowl and set aside. Cut cucumbers into slices or chunks. Add cucumbers, onion, and green pepper to tomatoes; drizzle with olive oil and toss.

In a small bowl, combine vinegar, sugar, salt and pepper. Pour vinegar mixture over salad and toss. Season to taste with salt and pepper.

Southern Potato Salad

Serves 10-12

This is my mother-in-law's recipe. Bobbie is a great southern cook who never measures or writes recipes down. So, I was happy when she agreed to make the potato salad while I measured every ingredient to ensure that we got the proportions just right. You know they say every great cook leaves something out of their recipes as to not give away their secrets, but this tastes pretty perfect to me. –Susie

5 pounds	Yukon Gold potatoes, peeled & diced
5	hard boiled eggs, divided
1 cup	mayonnaise
½ cup	onion, finely chopped
½ cup	celery, finely chopped
½ cup	sweet salad cubes
1 teaspoon	vinegar
2 teaspoons	sugar
	Salt & pepper, to taste
	Paprika, to garnish

Place potatoes in a large pot and cover with water. Bring water and potatoes to a boil and continue to boil for 20-25 minutes, until fork tender. Drain potatoes and spread them on a cookie sheet to cool.

In a large bowl, mash 3 hard boiled eggs with a fork, and add the remaining ingredients stirring until blended. Gently fold in potatoes. Season to taste with salt and pepper.

Place salad in serving bowl. Slice the remaining 2 eggs. Garnish the top of the salad with eggs and paprika.

Laura Says...
Create a
Recipe
Legacy

Do yourself a favor… take a minute, pick up the phone and call your mom, your aunt, your grandmother, your mother-in-law, or anyone whose cooking you enjoy, and ask them for their recipe that is your most favorite. Most likely, they will be flattered! Even better, if they wouldn't mind, ask them to write it out for you. My favorite recipes are those handwritten on index cards by my own grandmother. They are always delicious, and when I fix them, I feel as if she is there with me. –Laura

Skillet Baked Beans

Serves 10-12

This baked bean recipe is a cash prize worthy combo of mine and Laura's sister, Marcie's, and I must say "they are fabulous!" –Susie

7	bacon strips
1	large onion (1 cup), chopped
1	(53 ounce) can pork & beans
1 cup	ketchup
2 tablespoons	mustard
1 cup	dark brown sugar

Preheat oven to 350 degrees.

Chop three strips of bacon and place in a large 10-inch cast iron skillet. Over medium heat, cook bacon until it begins to render some fat; add the onion to the pan, and continue to cook until onion is translucent.

Remove skillet from heat. In the skillet, add beans, ketchup, mustard, and brown sugar. Cut the remaining 4 strips of bacon into thirds and neatly place them on top of the beans.

Place skillet in preheated oven and bake for 40-60 minutes, or until beans are thick, hot, and bubbly. Allow to cool a bit before serving.

An Unlikely Dip

Set a cast iron skillet of baked beans out with a bowl of chips when watching a ball-game or when you host a crowd. Watch as they devour the baked beans with gusto. Who knew baked beans could be a dip?

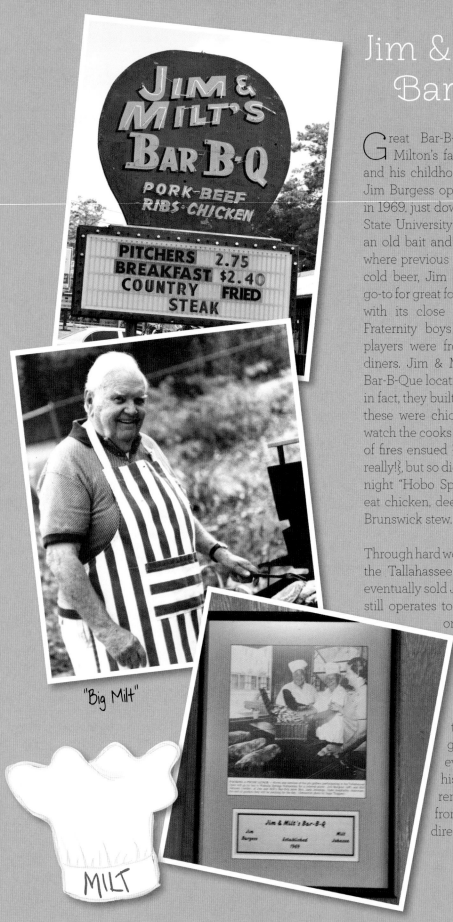

Jim & Milt's Bar-B-Q

Great Bar-B-Que is synonymous with Milton's family. Big Milt {Milton's dad} and his childhood friend and brother-in-law, Jim Burgess opened Jim & Milt's restaurant in 1969, just down the street from the Florida State University football stadium. Located in an old bait and tackle shop/honky-tonk bar, where previous owners sold live crickets and cold beer, Jim & Milt's quickly became the go-to for great food in Tallahassee, particularly with its close proximity to the university. Fraternity boys waited tables and football players were frequent {notoriously hungry} diners. Jim & Milt's was the only open pit Bar-B-Que location in the southeast for years... in fact, they built an open kitchen, long before these were chic, so those passing by could watch the cooks grill over the pit. Lots and lots of fires ensued {a firetruck was often called... really!}, but so did delicious food. The Tuesday night "Hobo Special" featured all you could eat chicken, deep fried corn and homemade Brunswick stew.

Through hard work and lots of late night hours, the Tallahassee icon was established. They eventually sold Jim & Milt's, but the restaurant still operates today, in the same location, as one of the oldest restaurants in town and features many of the original recipes.

As the years went by, Big Milt eventually passed the grilling tongs along to the next generation, happily teaching everyone at family cookouts his many tricks. He always remained "King of the Grill", and from the sidelines, energetically directed the timing to a tee!

"Big Milt"

MILT

BBQ Chicken

Serves 10

Actually, this recipe was given to us by Milton's older sister, Gail, whose grilling skills are the best in the Johnson family, {sorry, Milt!}. Fortunately, just as Big Milt taught her his secrets to grilling perfect Bar-B-Que chicken, she passed the family legacy on to Little Milt.   –Susie

10	half chickens
3 tablespoons	vegetable oil
1 teaspoon	garlic powder
	Salt & freshly ground pepper
1 cup	water
1 cup	white vinegar
	Big Milt's Basic BBQ Sauce (see page 34)

Thoroughly wash chicken, rub with vegetable oil, and generously cover with garlic powder, salt and pepper. In a spray bottle, mix water and white vinegar.

Prepare and light the grill.

Cook chicken on grill over low, indirect heat with hood down for approximately 50 minutes. Flip chicken 4 times while cooking, spraying chicken with vinegar mixture each time chicken is flipped. During last 10 minutes of cooking, baste with Bar-B-Que sauce and grill over direct heat.

Note: Chicken is done when you wiggle leg bone and it moves easily.

"Little Milt"

Making a Mop

Big Milt would always use his homemade "mops" to apply his famous sauce on anything he was grilling. They are easy to make and can be created from items found in your closet. Grab a wire hanger and a clean, new rag {about 12" square}. Clip off the bottom portion of the wire hanger and place the rag onto center of wire. Bend wire in half and twist so the rag hangs down. This mop allows you to generously apply sauce and the best part... dispose after use!

Big Milt's Basic BBQ Sauce

Yields 5 cups

Lucky for Laura, her husband grew up surrounded by Bar-B-Que masters. Lucky for us, Big Milt has left behind this recipe for his Basic Bar-B-Que Sauce. It is delicious and simple to make. –Susie

1 (28 ounce)	bottle store bought original recipe Bar-B-Que sauce (pick your favorite)
16 ounces	white vinegar
1	large sweet onion, coarsely sliced
2	stalks celery (leaves included), washed & coarsely chopped
1 tablespoon	Worcestershire sauce
3-4 good shakes	Louisiana-style hot sauce
½ teaspoon	garlic powder
2 tablespoons	vegetable oil
1 teaspoon	salt
½ teaspoon	pepper
2	lemons, halved & seeded

Pour the bottle of Bar-B-Que sauce into saucepan. Pour vinegar into the empty bottle. Shake to blend with remaining sauce and pour into saucepan.

Add onion, celery, Worcestershire, hot sauce, garlic powder, oil, salt and pepper. Squeeze lemon juice into saucepan and drop lemon halves into pan.

While stirring, bring to a boil. Cover and simmer for 2 hours.

Sauce will keep for up to one month refrigerated.

Note: If you like a sweeter sauce, add 2 tablespoons of brown sugar.

Saucy Gifts

Don't be afraid to make an extra large batch of this recipe when you are making sauce for a crowd... it's just as easy to make a big batch as it is to make a single recipe. Select a glass bottle - easily found online - and create custom labels tailored to your event. Your guests will love going home with the saucy secret!

Fluffy White Frosting

Sometimes I slice the layers of the Chocolate Chocolate Cake in half and spread each layer with this marshmallow like filling. Then, frost the cake with the chocolate frosting as usual.
–Susie

Place 2 egg whites in a mixing bowl and set aside for 15 minutes. In a saucepan over medium-high heat, stir 1 cup of water and ⅓ cup sugar until it comes to a boil. Using an electric mixer, beat egg whites, ¼ teaspoon cream of tartar, a pinch of salt and 1 teaspoon pure vanilla extract on high until soft peaks form. Reduce speed to medium and gradually add hot syrup; increase to high and mix for 7-10 minutes until stiff glossy peaks form. This makes enough frosting to ice a chocolate sheet cake.

Chocolate Chocolate Cake

Serves 10

Dee loves chocolate cake with chocolate icing so that is what we made her for her birthday. The cake part of the recipe is my great grandmother's. She swore that you could make it without eggs, but always threw the yolks in because she needed the egg whites for her Fluffy White Frosting. –Susie

	Non-stick baking spray with flour
2 ½ cups	all-purpose flour
1 teaspoon	baking soda
⅛ teaspoon	salt
1 cup	sugar
1 cup	light brown sugar, packed
½ cup	natural unsweetened cocoa powder
12 tablespoons	(1 ½ sticks) butter, unsalted
¾ cup	coffee (or water)
1 teaspoon	vanilla extract
2	eggs, whisked
1 cup	buttermilk

Preheat oven to 350 degrees and adjust oven rack to middle position. Use non-stick baking spray with flour to prepare two 9-inch round cake pans.

In a medium bowl, mix flour, baking soda and salt until blended. In medium sauce pan, add both sugars, cocoa, butter, and coffee and stir over medium heat until butter is melted and sugar is dissolved. Remove from heat and add vanilla.

Transfer warm chocolate to mixing bowl. Using electric mixer on medium-high speed, beat chocolate while gradually adding whisked eggs. Reduce mixer speed to medium low and add flour mixture while alternating with the buttermilk, beating just until blended after each addition. Finish by hand, using rubber spatula to incorporate all flour, because over beating can cause the cake to be tough.

Divide batter between two pans. Place cake pans in oven and bake for 30 minutes or until toothpick inserted in center comes out clean. Remove from oven and place on a rack to cool.

When bottom of cake pans are cooled run knife around edges to loosen cake from pan. Carefully invert cake onto serving plate. Spread cake with ½ cup chocolate frosting. Repeat removal procedure and frost top and sides of cake. Cake can be made ahead, covered and kept at room temperature.

Frosting:

10 tablespoons	(1 ¼ sticks) butter, unsalted
1 ¼ cups	light brown sugar, packed
1 cup	natural unsweetened cocoa powder
¼ teaspoon	salt
1 cup	heavy cream
2 teaspoons	vanilla extract

Place butter in medium saucepan and melt over medium-low heat. Whisk in sugar, cocoa powder and salt; stir until blended. Gradually whisk in cream. Using heat proof spatula, stir mixture until it is very hot and bubbles begin to form at edges; this process may take 5-10 minutes. Reduce heat to low and stir for 2 minutes. Remove from heat and stir in vanilla. {It will look like hot fudge sauce.} Transfer frosting to glass bowl and allow to rest for 15 minutes until cooled.

Refrigerate for 1 ½ hour, stirring every 30 minutes. Remove from refrigerator, stir and keep at room temperature.

Florida Lobster Feast

*Indulging in
surf & turf while
swapping tales
captured in the
Florida Keys*

Indulging in surf & turf...

Susie and I have both been lobstering since we were kids {long before we knew one another} taking similar trips to the Florida Keys with our families to experience a piece of paradise each year during lobster season. Located {seemingly} just steps from Miami, the Keys were a personal playground where we enjoyed the 'don't worry, be happy' atmosphere.

Susie and I both wanted our kids to experience the beauty and local color of life in the Keys - one of the few destinations where the simple charms of 'Old Florida' still exist. So we began the tradition of an annual Florida Lobster vacation with family friends several years back. Picture eight adults plus eight teenage children packed in cars full of groceries and gear, ready for the nine-hour drive south through Florida. Long before we even get close to "Mile Marker 80-something", we all start crafting our lobster seeking strategies and waging bets on which crustacean team will capture the most lobster loot.

"Nothing makes a lobster bigger than almost being caught."
-Milton Johnson

Our days are far from low-key; our boats leave the dock prior to the sun's arrival and only return after a long, successful day on the reef. At night, our lobster-stuffed bellies rally to play countless, cut-throat games of Guesstures, Ping Pong and Gin, with only a small amount of cheating. Our boats {and souls} are full as we make memories with our children. It's funny, no matter how hard we go while we're there, we are more relaxed than ever.

The anticipation of our annual adventure starts early... though we don't depart until the end of July! These pages offer a peek into our "pre-lobster trip" dinner where we gather together to reminisce about the past years' trips, fret about the lobsters that got away, look over funny photos and rehash numerous stories, all while working our strategies and planning for the next big hunt. You can bet that Florida lobster is always on the menu!

In Your Own Backyard

Using what's around you to create clever, yet simple décor elements

For our Florida-themed party, citrus was an absolute must. Not only is the variety of color cheerful and welcoming, the assembly is a breeze. The best part is that you can add these to your grocery list and pick them up as you're shopping for the event - one less stop! Leftover citrus can be juiced and frozen for quick and easy use in recipes.

A single palm frond can make a simple, yet dramatic statement with little effort on your part. I frequently place these branches in vases throughout my home. They last a long time and I am thankful that they are plentiful around our home. You can also allow palm fronds to dry out and turn brown - perfect for use in fall or rustic arrangements mixed with leafless branches and pine cones.

Decorating with glass jars is one of my favorite techniques. It's fun to fill up differently-shaped glass jars with seasonal items such as fruits, vegetables, nuts, berries, leaves, candies and countless other items that can be found in your own yard or pantry. The options are endless!

I often use orchids, which are abundantly grown with ease in Florida. I always love an excuse to buy these low maintenance beauties. They also make for an elegant, cheerful and sophisticated addition to any space. I most look forward to enjoying the blooms in my home, long after the party has come and gone... the longevity makes them worth every penny, and I never regret the cheer that they add to my days. Position potted orchids in the important focal areas of your party, then disperse them throughout your home near natural, indirect sunlight for everyday enjoyment.

Fish-filled Beginnings

Susie and I share many common memories from our Floridian upbringings, one of the many reasons that we are such good friends today. Most of all, we love swapping stories of our childhood Keys' adventures... wondering if our paths ever crossed.

The Florida Keys are a chain of islands separating the Gulf of Mexico from the Atlantic Ocean, each connected by one, often only two-lane, road. Childhood trips with family and friends to the "cabin" on Black Water Sound in Key Largo were community living at its finest. No air conditioning, one main living area where beds, couches and chairs served as sleeping quarters for many adults and children alike. There was one bathroom for countless overnight guests... with one light switch that turned on the overhead light in the sleeping area. Late night trips to the bathroom were a real treat for everyone else trying to get a little shut-eye!

Our days started with fishing for Snapper and Grunts off of the coral rocks behind our cabin. I learned to fish using live shrimp and bobbers, although it took a while to gather the courage to grab one of those living things and place it on my hook. The mangroves grabbed relentlessly at our hooks, and our moms patiently helped us untangle the lines to get them back in the water... so we had plenty to eat that night.

A short boat ride east through the beautiful mangrove channels took us into the unbelievably blue water of the Atlantic. We'd point our boat to one of the many coral reefs to dive and sometimes head beyond the reefs, to try our luck at offshore fishing in the nearby Gulf Stream.

- Laura

From when I was very small until I went off to college, one of our family vacations included a motley crew made up of aunts, uncles, cousins and friends traveling down to Islamorada in the Florida Keys for the Sportsman Season {amateur, mini lobster season}. The Pines and Palms, Siesta Motel or Smuggler's Cove had the pleasure of our company. Much like our present-day trips, we would lobster all day... eat fresh {usually steamed} lobster with Aunt Sandra's garlic bread at night and finish the evening with my mom's {could be famous} Key lime pie. The adults would sit around telling jokes and stories while the kids swam in the saltwater pool until bedtime... or until our parents drug us out on the boat again for night lobstering - from midnight until dawn.

The annual, unspoken competition between my dad and Uncle George was to "build the better mouse trap". Dad worked tirelessly before our trips on his boat-mounted waterproof lights for lobstering in the dark, only to arrive in the Keys to be out done. We would putter up onto the grassy flats at night and lower our lights into the water. Then, as the boat moved around slowly, we would seize the chance to bully net the lobster from the boat. Well, usually from the boat, unless you missed it and then out of frustration someone would jump overboard {my dad or brother} and go after the lobster on foot in the pitch black across the grassy flat... never good!

- Susie

Our Florida Lobster trips are a bit more comfortable these days as the Keys have tidied up a bit and we don't make all 16 guests sleep in the same room, but the traditions continue as we share with our own children our love for Florida fishing!

All Keyed Up!

At the end of each trip, I always ask all of the girls and our friends to share their most cherished moments. Some of my favorites from this past year:

The cry of "who has my mask?" as everyone tries to suit up and jump in and the promises of a Sharpie pen on board next year. *-Lynn*

Trying every conch fritter and Key Lime Pie that the Keys has to offer! *-Susie*

All of the "firsts"... the first dive of the first morning and the first bite into lobster tail that first evening. *-Kyle*

Our 2010 theme song, "Lobsternaire," sung to the tune of "Billionaire" and only complete when accompanied by our choreographed dance moves that we performed for our parents! *-Mary Parker*

Driving across Alligator Alley {with a prize for the first alligator sighting!} and fully appreciating the beauty of our state, wondering what the first settlers thought when they came upon it. The excitement that you feel the minute you arrive and step out of the car to the hot, humid, salty air, anticipating the week ahead. And the contrasting melancholy you feel when the last suitcase is loaded up and the car door slams shut and you pull out of the driveway for the last time - until next year. *-Lynn*

Spending time with the kids... most of it enjoyable! *-Kiff*

Kiff and I are the best team ever for lobstering... it gets pretty competitive down there! *-SaraKate*

Watching all of the girls make great appetizers; adults experimenting with new tropical drinks; how everyone is involved in making the dinners and of course, the games after dinner... and all of the laughter. *-Milton*

Eating like kings... far better than in any restaurant. Oh, and trying for six months to get the song "Billionaire" out of my head. Oh no, there it goes again. *-Ed*

menu

Not a Care in the World
Rum Runners

Roasted Red Pepper Lavosh

Spinach & Summer
Berry Salad

Potato Tortilla

Grilled Florida Lobster Tails

Whole Beef Tenderloin

Lemon Cheesecake with
Chocolate Crust

Named after the actual felonious "rum runners" that were among the first inhabitants of the Florida Keys, this cocktail was invented at the Holiday Isle Tiki Bar in the late 1950s. A new bartender discovered an overstock of Hirim Walker Blackberry Brandy, banana liqueur and light rum, so he packed this fruity cocktail with more than a little punch! The famed Holiday Isle was always notable as a slightly naughty place to go... wild things tend to happen when one partakes of too many Rum Runners!

Take Me to a Tiki

Many accessible by boat and car alike, Tiki bars are found all over the Florida Keys. We frequent these breezy, character-filled locales after a long day on the water and we love to partake in the creatively concocted cocktails... which Kiff often recreates back at our house!

Not a Care in the World Rum Runners

Serves 8, Yields 4 ½ cups

Once we arrive home from our long day of boating, our friend Kiff is our appointed bartender for the cocktail hour. He often experiments with various ingredients to make delicious, fresh tasting cocktails perfect for the occasion. This Rum Runners recipe he shares with us here is tasty and the perfect start to the evening festivities. –Susie

1 ½ cups	spiced rum
1 ½ cups	orange juice
½ cup	banana liqueur
½ cup	blackberry brandy
¼ cup	grenadine
¼ cup	pineapple juice
8	fresh pineapple wedges, to garnish

In a pitcher, pour rum, orange juice, banana liqueur, blackberry brandy, grenadine, and pineapple juice; stir to combine. Fill eight 12-ounce glasses with ice, and garnish with a pineapple wedge. Pour punch over ice and serve.

Note: The best part is the pineapple wedge after it has soaked awhile in the punch. I know it is hard to resist, but you will be glad if you save it for last!

Caroline and Handley enjoying some conch fritters at the tiki hut!

Roasted Red Pepper Lavosh

Serves 10-12

This is our friend Lynn's recipe, one she brings over every time we ask... which is every time she comes. Fabulous! If you can't find cracker bread, ask your specialty grocery or wine store to order it for you. There is a company, Valley Lavosh, out of Fresno, California and it retails for less than fifteen dollars for four big disks. Get creative when topping these and try things like caramelized onions, capers or olives. I like to serve Lavosh with {good store-bought} warmed marinara. –Susie

1	large piece lavosh cracker bread
1	(4 ounce) package soft goat cheese
2 cups	cheese, grated (Mexican or Italian 4 cheese blend)
1	(12 ounce) jar roasted red peppers, sliced into strips
½	bunch fresh cilantro, chopped
	Dried seasonings of choice

Preheat oven to 400 degrees and position oven rack to middle position.

Spread cracker bread with a generous amount of soft goat cheese. Top with grated cheese and roasted red peppers. Sprinkle with cilantro and dried seasonings.

Bake at 400 degrees directly on oven rack, until cheese melts and starts to bubble.

Note: The plain version is just 2 cups of Havarti on the cracker bread with pepper and/or herbs.

From the Curious Cook...

We have a tradition... whoever visits Tampa before our Keys trip must bring back crab rolls from a Cuban restaurant in the famed Ybor City neighborhood... perhaps The Tropicana or Brocato's, but my favorite is Carmine's! We pick them up uncooked and freeze them until our trip. These are made from Cuban bread stuffed with crab filling. Amazing - and must be served with hot sauce much like the Crab or Corn Fritter (see page 239) - they just taste better with hot sauce. I don't know who likes these more... me or Laura's husband, Milton. I always joke that I would leg wrestle him for the last crab roll... I could eat one everyday with a 1905 Salad from the famed Tampa eatery, The Columbia Restaurant. –Susie

Spinach & Summer Berry Salad

Serves 10-12

When making this salad, I use ripe summer strawberries, but any berries will do. Chop up fresh herbs and a little finely minced jalapeño, and all the guests will ask "what's so great in the salad?" –Susie

Dressing:

⅓ cup	raspberry white wine vinegar
2 tablespoons	olive oil
4 teaspoons	honey
¼ teaspoon	salt
¼ teaspoon	black pepper

Salad:

10 cups	fresh baby spinach (1 pound), washed & dried
2 cups	fresh strawberries (1 pint), sliced
2 cups	fresh pineapple (approx. ½), peeled & cubed
1	Granny Smith apple, cored & sliced
1	small red onion, thinly sliced (optional)
1 teaspoon	fresh jalapeño pepper, seeded & minced (optional)
¼ cup	flat-leaf fresh parsley or other herbs, chopped (optional)

In a small bowl, combine vinegar, oil, honey, salt and pepper. Whisk until blended and set aside. In large salad bowl, place spinach, strawberries, pineapple, apple, and red onion. Sprinkle with jalapeños and chopped herbs. Toss with desired amount of dressing and serve.

Potato Tortilla

Serves 12

Potato Tortilla can be served hot from the skillet, but is most impressive turned out and cut into wedges. It is delicious with beef, lobster or pork, and when accompanied by Verde Sauce {see page 59}, it is even more exceptional. This recipe has proven to be one of the most requested and a popular dish with kids and adults alike.. –Susie

½ cup	olive oil, divided
2 ½ pounds	Yukon Gold or red potatoes, peeled & thinly sliced
1 ½ cups	onion (approx. 2 medium), thinly sliced
10	eggs
	Kosher salt & black pepper, to taste
	Extra-virgin olive oil

Place sliced potatoes in large bowl with cool water to prevent them from turning brown.

Heat ¼ cup oil in a large cast iron skillet (10-inch or larger) or oven-safe, non-stick skillet over medium heat. Drain potatoes and place potatoes and onions in hot pan with oil. Generously season potato mixture with salt and pepper and sauté 20 minutes or more until potatoes and onions are soft and tender, but not brown.

In large bowl, whisk eggs and season them generously with salt and pepper. Pour cooked potato mixture in bowl and toss.

Adjust oven rack to the second from the top position and preheat the broiler to high.

Clean original skillet and heat ¼ cup of olive oil over medium heat. Pour the potato and egg mixture into the hot skillet. Allow tortilla to cook for one minute before covering and adjusting the heat to low. Cook covered for 20 minutes until the tortilla is almost set. Remove from stove and place tortilla in oven and broil until golden. Remove from oven and allow tortilla to rest for at least 5 minutes. Use spatula to loosen edges and bottom. Use care when inverting tortilla on serving platter.

From the
Curious Cook...
Spanish Tapa

I discovered Potato Tortilla during a visit to Spain, and by the end of our trip, I was convinced that this could be the country's national dish. *Tortilla de patatas* is a thick egg omelette made with potatoes and fried in lots of olive oil. In Spain, a wedge of tortilla is often served hot for breakfast and in a *bocadillo* {a sandwich made with crusty bread}, or in the evening, at room temperature as a *tapa* with a big glass of chilled white wine.

–Susie

Grilled Florida Lobster Tails

Serves 12

When entertaining, it is nice to serve guests something they don't eat everyday and eating lobster makes any seafood lover happy! We are spoiled here in Florida because almost every seafood market sells lobster tails. They are easy to cook and aren't as expensive as one might think.   –Susie

6-12	spiny lobster tails
8 tablespoons	(1 stick) butter, melted
2	garlic cloves, minced
¼ cup	fresh flat-leaf parsley or cilantro, finely chopped
	Salt & black pepper
2	lemons, to garnish
	Verde Sauce (see page 59)
	Bamboo skewers

If lobster tails are frozen, place tails in bowl and thaw in refrigerator overnight.

Prepare and light grill. Using a large butcher knife, cut the lobster tails in half lengthwise. Remove dark vein, if any. Rinse lobster pieces under cool water and pat dry. Thread bamboo skewers through halved lobster tails so they won't curl while cooking on the grill.

In a small saucepan over medium heat, melt butter. Remove saucepan from heat and stir garlic, herbs, and a pinch of salt and pepper into melted butter. Brush lobster tails with garlic butter and grill for 10-15 minutes, or just until the shell is pink and the meat is opaque.

Serve with lemon wedges and Verde Sauce (see page 59).

Note: Before purchasing lobster, decide if you will serve your guest a half or whole lobster tail. If serving lobster tails along with Grilled Tenderloin plan to serve a half of a lobster tail per person. If serving lobster alone, serve one whole lobster tail per person.

From the Curious Cook... Keep It Fresh

When we catch lobster, we like to freeze them in ocean water. Laura and Milton insist on cruising out into the bluest water to fetch buckets of clear water for lobster freezing. No water from the marina, for sure! I swear… they taste as good as the day we caught them if they're frozen in fresh saltwater.   –Susie

The hunt for Lobster...

Our crew prefers to snorkel for lobster, versus scuba diving. Snorkelers - donning masks, snorkels, fins, gloves, tickle sticks, nets and bags - work in teams {except Milton who is much happier working alone as he is often NOT a team player}. The method is to slowly swim along, keeping your eyes peeled for rocks or ledges where the lobsters hide. There is often more than one lobster in a hole {if you're lucky, there are lots}, and you can spy them as their antennae stick out, waving in the water. The team should be "at the ready" once lobsters are spotted. The first person, "the tickler," dives down and uses a long "tickle stick" to coax the lobster from his hole, encouraging their signature territorial nature and bringing them out ready for a fight. At this point, the second half of the team, "the netter," should be ready to scoop them up from behind. Fortunately, we have somewhat of an advantage as lobster only swim backward, but they are fast, so the netter must be ready to "catch hell" if they lose the lobster... much ribbing and criticism most certainly will ensue.

Lobstering is VERY competitive so occasionally we forget that it's a team effort. We won't name names, however there was a particularly famous

shouting/wrestling match over who was going to get a particular lobster, resulting in lost equipment {net, tickle stick, etc.}, luckily discovered later by a passing swimmer.

The Florida Lobster season begins August 1st, but an 'insider's tip' is to go during Sportsman Season, which is the last Wednesday and Thursday in July. This gives the amateur lobster catcher an advantage over professional trappers.

Plan to spend much time in the strategy of the "hunt for lobster." We study charts, pull up favorite numbers in the GPS and spend a good deal of time scouting ahead. Above all, be prepared for the lobster prize pool... everyone takes a stab at how many total lobster will be caught, with the closest guesstimate winning the grand prize money pool. It makes me happy to see the personalities of our group shine here - some choose zero {pessimists!} and others select overly ambitious, nearly impossible numbers.

 - Laura

Whole Beef Tenderloin

Serves 10-12

Everyone should learn this easy technique for cooking whole beef tenderloin. You must have a meat thermometer, but the steps are simple, and the results are sure to impress your crowd.   –Susie

1	whole beef tenderloin (5-6 pounds), trimmed & tied
3	garlic cloves, sliced lengthwise into 4 pieces each
⅓ cup	olive oil, divided
2 tablespoons	peppercorns
2 tablespoons	kosher salt
2 tablespoons	granulated garlic
	Verde Sauce

Using a small paring knife, cut slits in tenderloin and stuff with small slivers of garlic. Brush beef with 2 tablespoons of olive oil.

Place peppercorns, salt and granulated garlic in spice grinder and process, or place in mortar and crush with pestle. Cover meat with seasoning. Allow meat to sit at room temperature for at least 30 minutes before preheating oven.

Preheat oven to 500 degrees and adjust oven rack to middle position.

Heat a large oven proof skillet over medium-high to high heat. Put 3 tablespoons olive oil in pan and immediately place seasoned tenderloin in hot pan. Sear tenderloin quickly on all sides until nicely browned. Insert meat thermometer in tenderloin so it can be read through oven door. Place skillet with tenderloin in oven and bake only 5 minutes. Turn oven off and leave skillet in oven for approximately 10 more minutes, or until meat reaches 125 degrees or desired temperature. (See chart below)

120-125 degrees F = Medium rare
130-140 degrees F = Medium
150 degrees F = Well done

Remove tenderloin from oven, with the understanding it will continue to cook after removing from oven. Allow the meat to stand for 5-10 minutes before carving into ¼ - ½-inch slices. Serve with Verde Sauce (see side bar for recipe) or horseradish sauce.

Simple Seasoning

The seasoning for the beef tenderloin is also excellent for flavoring grilled steaks. Place equal parts peppercorns, kosher salt and granulated garlic in mortar and crush with pestle. Make plenty, so that you'll always have some on-hand.

Verde Sauce

In a food processor, place 1½ cups fresh cilantro, ⅔ cup fresh mint, 4 chopped green onions (white and light green parts), 2 tablespoons seeded and minced jalapeño, 6 minced garlic cloves, 3 teaspoons lime zest, juice of 1 lime, 2 tablespoons honey and 1 teaspoon sea salt; process. Stop to scrape side and gradually add ⅔ cup olive oil until blended.

Sour Cream Topping

Spoon mounds of sour cream on top of cheesecake and use a spatula to smooth. Return cake to oven and bake for an additional 5 minutes. Remove cheesecake from oven and run a sharp knife around the edge of pan to loosen cake. Immediately refrigerate cheesecake, uncovered and still in pan, overnight.

When ready to serve, release the sides of the springform pan, and run a sharp knife between the crust and pan to loosen. Transfer cheesecake to cake plate and garnish the top of the cake with chocolate and lemon slices.

Lemon Cheesecake with Chocolate Crust

Serves 10–12

Lynn first brought this cheesecake to one of my dinner parties. It was so fabulous I dreamed about it later that night, and the next morning I regretted not eating more. So when the opportunity presents itself, I'll always have an extra-large piece of this cheesecake. –Susie

Crust:
	Non-stick baking spray with flour
6 tablespoons	all-purpose flour
1 ½ teaspoons	special dark cocoa powder
⅛ teaspoon	salt
4 tablespoons	(½ stick) unsalted butter
3 ounces	bittersweet chocolate, chopped
¾ cup	sugar
¼ cup	light brown sugar, packed
1	egg, beaten
1 teaspoon	vanilla extract

Filling:
5	(8 ounce) packages cream cheese, room temperature
1 ¾ cups	sugar
2 tablespoons	all-purpose flour
1 tablespoon	lemon peel, finely grated
6 teaspoons	fresh lemon juice
5	eggs
2	egg yolks
½ cup	sour cream
¼ cup	heavy whipping cream

Topping:
1 ½ cups	sour cream
	Bittersweet chocolate, chopped or shaved
1	lemon, halved lengthwise, thinly sliced crosswise

Crust:

Preheat oven to 350 degrees and adjust oven rack to middle position. Prepare 9-inch diameter springform pan with non-stick baking spray. In a small bowl, combine flour, cocoa, and salt; set aside.

Place butter in large saucepan and heat over medium-low heat until melted. Remove from heat and add chopped chocolate. Whisk until smooth.

Whisk both sugars into chocolate, and set mixture aside to cool for 10 minutes. When mixture has cooled, add egg and vanilla to chocolate and whisk until blended. Gradually add flour mixture to chocolate mixture and stir until combined. Pour chocolate batter into prepared pan.

Bake the crust for 20 minutes or until it starts to crack. Place on rack and allow crust to cool for 30 minutes or until room temperature. Keep oven at 350 degrees.

Filling:
In a large bowl, using an electric mixer, beat cream cheese until smooth. Add sugar, flour, lemon peel, lemon juice, and mix thoroughly. One at a time, add eggs and yolks, beating until combined after each addition. Add ½ cup of sour cream and ¼ cup of whipping cream; beat until creamy. Pour filling over chocolate crust in pan and use a spatula to level surface prior to baking.

Place pan on a rimmed cookie sheet and bake for 1 hour 20 minutes or until cake is lightly golden and set around the edges. The center will move slightly when shaken. Remove from oven. Keep oven at 350 degrees. Continue with Sour Cream Topping instructions (on opposite page).

Al Fresco Dinner Party

Sharing tastes, toasts and travel tips for adventures abroad

Sharing tastes...

I met my husband Milton three short months before he asked me to marry him and though we hadn't known one another long, I knew that his southern charm and easygoing, patient disposition perfectly complemented my own fast-paced, artistic energy. While our brief courtship was a bit of a risk, the rewarding adventure of our marriage has been well worth the chance we took.

Fast-forward 25 years to find my sister and I both celebrating silver anniversaries with our husbands and our parents marking their 50th year of marriage... an adventure in Italy was most certainly in order. It would be the first tour to *la Penisola* for Milton and I, so we started our own celebration a bit before departure with a little *al fresco* affair, full of touring tips and toasts from our well-traveled friends.

> " The world cracks open for those willing to take a risk. "
>
> -Frances Mayes, *A Year in the World: Journeys of a Passionate Traveller*

Susie teamed up with our dear friend and favorite Aussie, Julz, to set the stage for the bon voyage event. Susie is well versed in the indulgent tempo of Italian dining, so she graciously prepared a flavorful meal, while Julz's beautifully eclectic, Mediterranean style home and relaxed Australian hospitality {not to mention her charming accent} created the perfect locale for a delicious dinner party full of good friends and memories.

Julz met her husband, Billy, in Sydney at the end of his five-year backpacking stint around the world... as quite possibly the only woman he had yet to date. With two pairs of skis, flip flops and a pack, he returned to the States only to have Julz follow him, promising her parents it would just be a 'quick holiday.' Twenty-four years of marriage later and living

life with gusto, Julz and Billy are an adventuresome couple, often traveling solo to pursue their individual passions. They immerse themselves in the culture when traveling, Billy researching his ventures thoroughly and Julz pretty much winging it and hoping for the best. The results are the same... big smiles and stories to share. Julz claims to have little talent in the kitchen {which isn't true whatsoever}, so when entertaining, she makes sure that what she thinks she lacks in the culinary department she makes up for in atmosphere, and of course, the number one rule - plentiful drinks and don't eat early. From Gilligan's Island dance parties on the beach to Swinging 50's Rat Pack cocktail parties, costumes are often mandatory, and it all starts with the invitation.

With the Prosecco flowing and surrounded by the warmth of great friends, our own *al fresco* send off certainly did not disappoint. Billy and Julz charmed with their hospitality; Susie presented a mouth-watering menu; and the evening was timed with an authentic Italian tempo... all creating the perfect setting for a night of feasting on memorable tales, great travel tips, fabulous tastes and above all, heart-warming toasts. A few days later, Milton and I left for our adventure, well prepared to experience Italy to its fullest. After our incredible trip, I returned home artistically inspired by Italy. Today, I still smile at the memories, seeing bits of inspiration from my travels tucked in the current Coton Colors collection.

Sharing Toasts...

Find a local wine merchant and allow them to be your go-to '*Vino Aficionado*.' Simply take your menu into the store and let the expert select the perfect Italian wines to accompany your menu flavors, even finding wines from the same regions from which your dish originates. Bring your overseas theme beyond the expectation of wine by serving Italian *birra* or select craft beers with labels lending well to the theme's décor. Garnish Italian Prosecco with seasonal fruit for a fresh addition to your bubbly toasts.

Authentic Italian Dining

...regardless of the coordinates of your locale

The Italian love affair with cuisine and their approach to daily dining as an event is truly inspiring. While many of us would consider three-hour, multi-course meals too much for an everyday cook to handle, our culture could take a lesson or two in savoring time and tastes from the Italians. While a lavish affair may be difficult to replicate with regularity, it is certainly an art worth imitating on occasion, taking it slow to enjoy both the process of cooking and the joy of eating.

Evoking an Italian feel at your own *al fresco*, 'in the fresh air', party can be accomplished with a few simple décor concepts and tastes of authenticity tied throughout your menu. Incorporate a few of these elements and your guests will immediately feel as if they are perched on an Italian *piazza* or on the steps of a Tuscan villa, overlooking olive trees and vineyards... no matter where your party takes place.

- Don't be afraid to bring your dining table outdoors to create a bit of casual elegance.

- Travel photos or wedding albums can evoke entertaining conversations amongst your guests. Ask your friends to bring an album from their favorite trip or from their own wedding, scatter about in seating areas and let the memory sharing begin.

- The simplest of door décor greets guests and sets the tone for the evening. Follow the lead of local *ristorante* owners in Italy and personally greet each of your guests at the door upon arrival.

- Stacking an array of fresh artisan bread loaves on the table makes for a surprisingly simple, yet tasteful table decoration, adding to the casual ambiance for the evening.

- Placecards can be very useful at parties with more than six guests, particularly as they allow you to control the conversation atmosphere according to individuality, while adding a personalized touch. The act of creating place cards does not have to be difficult or expensive. An artichoke in its raw form tied with a handwritten card or a wine cork cut to hold a small place card are simple ways to dictate the vibe of dinner chatter.

The recipes presented in this chapter are closely aligned with the rich culture to create an authentic, Italian meal with multiple courses. To simplify, you can select to serve just a few of the courses or choose to purchase prepared dishes to cut back on the cooking. No matter how you choose to create your own event, just be sure to slow down and enjoy the company of family and friends. As long as the pace is right and the wine is plentiful, your guests will certainly feel the essence of Italy.

A Gracious Hostess

In Julz' words...

I prefer to spend time in one place when traveling to really get the feel of the culture, immersing myself in the daily life, living in a tiny apartment away from the tourists and meeting many locals. I was even fortunate enough to receive an invitation to Frances Mayes' Italian villa, *Bramasole*, during one of my extended stays in Cortona. Alberto, a long-time Florida friend and neighbor to Frances brokered the invitation. I was excited to be included at the table of this author whose own 20-year love affair with Italy is well documented in her many books, including *Under the Tuscan Sun*. I was also well aware that my friend Alberto lived *la dolce vita* and that details were not so *importante*.

That evening, I knew something was amiss when {not another guest in sight}. I ventured up the grass driveway of the villa to see the most beautiful *al fresco* table setting overlooking the valley down to Lago Trasimeno. The double doors to the kitchen were wide open and with carefully selected wine in hand I ventured in, only to see Frances {whom I had never met} turn around with a look of surprised concern on her face. To which I stammered, "Frances, I am Julz, you know Alberto's friend." Silence... more silence. "Oh {pause}, we weren't expecting you."

Fast forward to discover that not only was I not expected, but the invited guests were not due to arrive for another hour. Recovering her poise, Frances graciously showed me through her home and around her sumptuous garden, at which point the *al fresco* dining table was rearranged to add another. As Michaelangelo's *Last Supper* is perfect already, so was Frances' table setting; squeezing in another place setting was the equivalent of painting in a 13th unknown disciple to the table... but she did, *Brava!* The night was perfection, the evening light pink and gold, the view, the conversation, the people and ah the food and wine... that warm Tuscan hospitality you read about. As Italians say... this is the life.

—Julz

> "We weren't expecting you."

Susie's Italian Adventure Tips

...some learned the hard way!

When traveling overseas, we Americans tend to be a bit wary of locals wanting to provide help or guidance in dining. Fortunately for my palate, I've learned to get past our hesitation and allow the Italians to share what they know best – the art of living and eating well. At one particular *trattoria* in Rome, there are no menus. "Mama" serves everyone in the restaurant the same meal, living up to the "Here you eat what we feed you" motto displayed at the entrance. From the lentils, fried rice balls, ham croquettes and marinated tomatoes to the roasted fresh pork, the meal there - where we had no say over what food was set before us and the only decision we had to make was red or white - was simply an experience my family will never forget. By the end of the evening, kisses abounded for all... "Mama" had welcomed our teenage daughter Kate with a kiss on the forehead and bid me farewell with two kisses - *Ciao* to new friends!

If your teenage son takes a sudden interest in his summer reading while on the beach, realize this likely has much more to do with the topless women enjoying the surf and less about his love of literature!

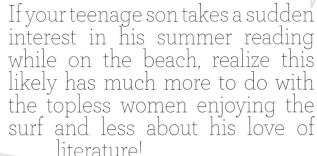

If happenstance ever takes you to Siena, keep your eyes peeled for a mounted boar's head donning sunglasses around the corner from the *Panforte* shop that sits on the *piazza*. Tucked just behind the landmark, you will find you the most delicious *Porchetta* sandwich. Order one {they are very large}, perch yourself alongside your travel companion on Il Campo and savor as you watch the Italian life pass you by. Important note – don't be tempted to sling open the beaded curtain to steal a photograph of the proprietor because he will promptly blast his blow horn in protest of paparazzi.

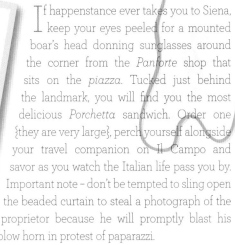

We first fell in love with the crisp Italian liquor, *Limoncello*, while visiting Venice. We'd spent an unusually extravagant day shopping on the island of Murano and as we toasted our purchases {rather, drowned our buyers' remorse}, the shopkeeper must have alerted the mayor of the neighboring island of Burano of our buying habits. The next thing we knew a high-speed boat whisked us over to the island where the mayor was there waiting on the dock happy to see us. Little did he know our budget was shot and our husbands were earlier threatening to fling themselves out the window but decided against it because the building was only two stories high. The township still extended their gracious hospitality and overwhelmed us with delectable cuisine. The owner of the local *ristorante* insisted that he "take care of you" and when, at the end of the meal, he inquired *"Limoncello?"*, we were so happy and trusted him totally. "What the heck. *Si*, why not!" He brought out small glasses and poured ice cold *Limoncello* and in the same moment, as if on cue, the music started and a lovely bride and what appeared to be the whole community merrily strolled down the street in front of us. As we sat there, we looked at each other and giggled... we could not believe how lucky we were. A true "thank you God... life is good" moment! Gone were the feelings of guilt and regret... it is amazing what a little sip of *Limoncello* will do. As the lovely afternoon drew to a close, we raised our glasses to the unexpected discoveries of our Italian adventure.

" Don't put gas in your diesel car... *enough said.* "

Don't be afraid to make new friends while traveling abroad. I recall Ed and I sharing a fun Italian drink – a lemon soda splashed with vodka and garnished with a watermelon wedge at a bar over looking the surf in Cinque Terre. Alongside a group of fun-loving Aussies, we exchanged restaurant recommendations and they actually told us about Mama's *trattoria* and the trendy Trastevere neighborhood.

Bring water shoes to wear in the surf in Monterosso al Mare, lest you prefer to crawl out like an old sea hag versus a graceful mermaid!

Most importantly, wherever your travels take you, bring back a small treasure to keep the memories with you for always. Don't be inclined to select perishable items like olive oil {though it is delicious}, and it needn't be the extravagance of a Murano glass chandelier. Whether choosing for yourself or a gift for a friend, select a simple token like lace from Burano, a leather tote, a handmade bowl or platter or a small piece of jewelry such as this one Kate found in Volterra. Do not be afraid to ship your purchases home {when traveling that should be your mantra anyway... do not be afraid... do not be afraid...} because it is never as expensive as you would think and you will be glad you have a souvenir to remember your trip. Ed and I eat olives most nights while cooking dinner, and I love the green ceramic olive bowl with the little pocket for the pits we purchased on a trip, it never fails to make me smile.

–Susie

menu

Eggplant Caponata

Cannellini Beans

Sicilian Meatballs

Marinara

Lemon Fettuccine

Herb Grilled Pork Chops

Italian Chopped Salad

Chocolate Truffles

Eggplant Caponata

Serves 8-12

The story goes that Caponata was originally served in the taverns of old Sicily. A traditional dish, Eggplant Caponata is especially good piled on either a piece of Bruschetta or Crostini. This hearty Antipasto is sure to satisfy. –Susie

¼ cup	olive oil
¾ cup	onion (approx. 1 medium), chopped
2	stalks celery, thinly sliced
4-5 cups	eggplant (approx. 1 large round), skin on, ½-inch diced
1	red pepper, ½-inch diced
1	(14.5 ounce) can diced tomatoes no salt added, drained
2	garlic cloves, minced
2 tablespoons	balsamic vinegar
1	lemon, zested & juiced
1 teaspoon	honey
¼ cup	golden raisins
¼ teaspoon	kosher salt
¼ teaspoon	coarsely ground black pepper
3 tablespoons	fresh basil, chopped & divided
	Toasted pine nuts, capers or kalamata olives (optional)

Bruschetta:

1 loaf	Italian bread, sliced
6	garlic cloves, cut in half
	Olive Oil
	Sea salt & pepper

Heat oil in large skillet over medium heat. Add onion and celery, and cook for 5 minutes until soft. Stir in eggplant, and cook for 8 minutes or until it starts to shine and not look dry. Add red pepper, tomatoes, and garlic. Stir, and gently cook for 15 minutes until the vegetables start to breakdown.

Add vinegar, lemon zest and juice, honey, raisins, salt and pepper. Reduce heat to medium-low, and gently cook for 10-15 minutes until all vegetables are soft and the caponata is stew-like and thick. Remove from heat and stir in 2 tablespoons of basil. Season to taste with salt and pepper. Drizzle with a touch of olive oil and sprinkle with remaining basil. Serve hot, warm, or room temperature. Garnish with pine nuts, capers, or olives, if desired.

Bruschetta vs. Crostini

It is the preparation technique that sets these two types of toast points apart. To prepare Bruschetta, either grill or toast slices of rustic Italian bread and then rub with fresh garlic cloves, drizzle with warm olive oil and top. In contrast, thinly slice a baguette to make Crostini, 'tiny toasts', and brush with olive oil prior to toasting. Either method perfectly accompanies this recipe or a variety of tasty Italian appetizers.

Herb Snips

Make sure your basil is dry before you chop or it might turn black. Susie uses scissors to snip basil and many other herbs like mint or parsley.

Bruschetta:
Rub slices of grilled Italian bread with garlic cloves. Drizzle the bread with olive oil and sprinkle with salt and pepper.

Cannellini Beans

Serves 8-10

Commonly used by Italian hosts to begin a meal, 'Buon Appetito' literally means "good appetite." The Italian appetizer - Antipasto - is simply meant to be a "mouth opener". Choose just a few simple dishes, such as this recipe, to tempt your guests' palate without overfilling. Legumes are popular and are served hot or cold throughout Italy. The combination of cannellini beans and sage in this recipe is one of my favorites because it is earthy and comforting. You can experiment with other seasonal herbs - such as rosemary, Italian parsley or dill.

–Susie

2	(15.5 ounce) cans cannellini beans
⅓ cup	fresh sage leaves, torn into small pieces
1	head of garlic
1 cup	white wine
¼ cup	olive oil
	Kosher salt & freshly ground black pepper
	Olive oil, to drizzle
	Bruschetta (see page 72-73)

Preheat oven to 400 degrees.

Drain, rinse and place beans in a small baking dish. Stir in sage and a pinch of black pepper {no salt yet}. Peel the outer skins off the head of garlic as much as possible, but make sure it will stay together whole. Cut the top off the head of garlic to expose the cloves. Place the head of garlic upright in center of beans. Pour wine over beans and drizzle with ¼ cup olive oil. Cover tightly with foil, cut small slit in foil, and bake for 1 hour or until beans are tender and flavorful.

Remove the garlic head, and place half the beans and all the juice in a bowl. Squeeze 6 cloves of roasted garlic into bowl and smash the beans and garlic together. Mix the remaining whole beans into the bean, sage, and garlic mixture. Allow beans to sit for 5 minutes to let flavors meld. Taste, then season with a dash of salt and plenty of pepper.

Pour beans into a serving dish and drizzle with olive oil. Serve with bruschetta. (see page 72-73)

Note: Feel free to use vegetable or chicken broth instead of wine.

Simple Starters

Italian cuisine offers a number of starters that can be purchased in advance, and with minimal prep work they are easily served in bowls scattered about from which your guests can nibble. Simple starter ideas include:

- Fresh cantaloupe, wrapped in thinly sliced prosciutto, drizzled with olive oil and topped with fresh, chopped mint

- Radishes, eggplant, red pepper or asparagus, doused with olive oil, sprinkled with salt and roasted in the oven or on the grill

- Frico cheese wafers, made by mounding freshly grated Parmesan on a parchment-lined cookie sheet, baked at 350 degrees for 4-5 minutes and cooled for 2 minutes. Serve with cured meats such as Salame or Mortadella

- Marinated olives, mushrooms, beans, baby artichokes and pickled mixed vegetables can all be purchased from your local grocery and simply served

- Fresh or dried figs, dried apricots, and pistachios with garlic are great choices for munching throughout the evening

Sicilian Meatballs

Serves 8 appetizers, 4 entrées

Tuna is a very popular and plentiful fish in Sicily, particularly because it is the island to which these fish swim to spawn. Make these meatballs, and be prepared to feast on something fabulous! –Susie

1 pound	fresh tuna, ½-inch diced
1 loaf	Cuban or Italian bread
1 teaspoon	cinnamon
¼ teaspoon	kosher salt
¼ teaspoon	black pepper
1 teaspoon	dried oregano
¼ cup	olive oil, divided
¼ cup	pine nuts
1 cup	fresh flat-leaf parsley, chopped & divided
¼ cup	Parmesan cheese, freshly grated
1	lemon, zested & juiced
2	eggs
2-4 cups	Marinara sauce (see page 79)

Preheat oven to 350 degrees.

Cube enough bread to make 2 cups of breadcrumbs, and place them on a baking sheet. Toast bread in oven for 3-4 minutes, turn oven off, and let bread dry out.

Use spice grinder or mortar and pestle to grind cinnamon, salt, pepper, and oregano together. Season fish with spice mixture. Heat 2 tablespoons of oil in large skillet over medium heat. Add fish and pine nuts. Sauté until the fish is cooked on all sides and the pine nuts are toasted. Remove from heat and place fish in large bowl to cool.

Pulse bread in food processor to make fine bread crumbs. Add 2 cups of breadcrumbs to fish. Set aside ¼ cup parsley for garnish. Add ¾ cup parsley, Parmesan, lemon juice and zest, eggs, and combine with hands. Wash hands. Dip hand into a bowl of cold water before forming meatballs. Roll meatballs to the size of a ping-pong ball. Place meatballs on an oiled tray, tightly cover with plastic wrap or foil, and place in refrigerator for at least an hour and up to 24 hours.

Continued...

Complementary Beverages

The evening's authenticity can carry through in the beverages served, even down to the water poured. Susie suggests serving mineral water {chilled, with "gas" and no ice} especially with seafood as the minerals in the water complement the fish well.

When ready to serve, bring 2 cups of marinara sauce to simmer. Heat 2 tablespoons of oil in large fry pan over medium heat. Add meatballs to pan and cook until nicely browned, approximately 3 minutes. These may be cooked in two batches, adding more oil between batches if necessary. Place cooked meatballs in marinara, and simmer until heated through. Garnish with ¼ cup parsley and a touch of olive oil.

If serving as an entrée: Use 4 cups of marinara, make the meatballs larger, and serve over pasta. Serve with freshly grated Parmesan.

Tool Tips

Don't be intimidated by using a mortar and pestle. Simply throw in your herbs, pepper and top with salt to easily grind your flavors for the dish. Invest in this tool... you'll use it over and over again!

Marinara

Yields 4 cups

A fresh made sauce with varying ingredients, Marinara originated in coastal Italian cities. From the Latin 'mar', which translates 'sea', the wives of fishermen made this pasta sauce traditionally with fresh tomatoes, garlic, olive oil and oregano to accompany the day's catch. –Susie

1 tablespoon	dried oregano
½ teaspoon	kosher salt
½ teaspoon	coarsely ground black pepper
2 tablespoons	olive oil
2 cups	onion (approx. 2 large), chopped
6	garlic cloves, minced
2	(28 ounce) cans whole peeled tomatoes (preferably San Marzano)
4 tablespoons	tomato paste
¼ cup	wine (whatever you are drinking or red wine vinegar)

Place oregano, salt and pepper in a spice grinder and process, or place in a mortar and use pestle to grind spices into a fine powder.

Heat oil in a large skillet over medium heat. Sauté the onions for 5 minutes. Add the garlic and cook for 3 minutes longer. Sprinkle with oregano, salt and pepper mixture and reduce heat to low. Pour juice of canned tomatoes in pan and stir.

Take a tomato from the can and hold it over the pan while pulling the soft red pulp away from the tough stem area. Let the tomato and juice fall into the pan. Dispose of the tough core. Repeat the process for the rest of the tomatoes. Make sure the temperature of the sauce is not too hot; use hands to finish crushing the tomatoes. Stir in tomato paste and wine, and then bring to a boil. Reduce heat to low and simmer for at least one hour, stirring occasionally until marinara is sweet and thick. Taste and add a pinch of salt, if needed.

Note: Marinara can be refrigerated for a week or frozen for months.

From the Curious Cook...

An admired Italian cook once told me to always grind the oregano because "you don't want it to look like you have dead flies floating on top of your marinara!" –Susie

Spicing it up a Notch

For a spicier rendition of this recipe - *all' Arrabbiata* or "angry style" - add six, chopped sweet cherry pickled peppers {partially seeded} when sautéing the onion and garlic. Continue through recipe steps as directed to create a hot Italian sauce with zing, perfect for serving over linguine or penne pasta. Be sure to add lots of fresh Parmesan. Be warned... the vibrant character of this sauce is not for the faint of palates!

Lemon Fettuccine

Serves 8

A more elegant alternative to the standard Fettuccine Alfredo, this recipe is an instant crowd pleaser and is simple enough for a weeknight meal. Kids love it!

–Susie

2 cups	heavy cream
2	lemons, zested & set lemons aside
3 tablespoons	fresh rosemary leaves, chopped & divided
1 pound	fettuccine
2 cups	pecorino or Parmesan cheese (6 ounces), freshly grated & divided
	Kosher salt and freshly ground black pepper

In a large pot, bring 8 cups of water with several pinches of kosher salt to a rolling boil. {Someone once told me "…pasta water should be salty like sea water."}

Add 2 cups of heavy cream to a large skillet over medium-low heat. Simmer and stir continuously until cream is reduced to almost half. Turn heat to low, add lemon zest and 2 tablespoons of chopped rosemary leaves to cream.

Add pasta to boiling water and cook just short of *al dente, to the tooth,* approximately 5-6 minutes. Using a pasta fork/spoon, transfer the damp hot pasta directly to the cream sauce. Add ½ cup of pasta water to sauce and toss. Squeeze juice of 1 lemon over pasta and top with a handful of the cheese and toss. Taste and add salt, plenty of black pepper, and possibly more lemon juice. Garnish with 1 tablespoon of chopped rosemary; serve immediately with remaining freshly grated cheese and pair with a big glass of wine.

Note: When purchasing Parmesan, buy a wedge of cheese and grate it yourself. This adds the freshest and most authentic taste to the dish.

Rosemary–Countless Uses for a Simple Herb

A heat-loving herb literally meaning "dew of the sea," Rosemary is associated with flavors of the Mediterranean. This herb is so easy to grow. The fragrance is lovely and it is difficult to kill… plant it and forget about it. Snip it from your kitchen garden as a garnish, in seasoning as you cook or simply tied for décor.

Herb Grilled Pork Chops

Serves 8

Pork steaks are my favorite cut to use for this recipe; they are usually about ½-inch thick and are fatty so they don't dry out while grilling However, any one-inch cut of the pork chop or a veal chop will work just as well... simply use plastic wrap and a mallet to pound to ½-inch thickness.   –Susie

8	center loin pork chops (8 ounce each), pounded to ½-inch thickness
½ cup	olive oil
	Lime zest (2 limes)
¼ cup	lime juice (approx. 2 limes)
6	garlic cloves, minced
½ cup	fresh flat-leaf parsley, chopped
¼ cup	fresh oregano leaves, chopped
¼ cup	fresh rosemary leaves, chopped
	Kosher salt & coarsely ground black pepper

Take chops out of refrigerator, and place in a large glass baking dish. Prepare and light the grill.

In a small bowl, mix rosemary, parsley, and oregano. Set aside ¼ cup for garnish.

Make marinade by whisking olive oil, lime zest, lime juice, and garlic together in another small bowl. Pour marinade over pork chops, and sprinkle both sides of chops with the remaining ¾ cup of herbs. Cover baking dish with plastic wrap, allowing chops to marinate in a cool spot for 20 minutes, but not in the refrigerator. *Do not marinate chops in lime juice mixture for longer than 20 minutes or have pork sit out at room temperature for more than 30 minutes.*

Generously salt and pepper chops before placing on the grill or hot grill pan. Grill 3 minutes per side or cook to your liking. Transfer pork chops to serving platter and top with extra chopped parsley, oregano, and rosemary.

Top with Italian Chopped Salad and enjoy! (see page 84)

Italian Chopped Salad

Serves 8

A tasty technique that I first learned in Spain... mix the dressing in the bottom of a wooden salad bowl, top with salad ingredients and wait until moments prior to serving to toss. This allows you to prepare the dish in advance, in a single bowl, without wilting the salad. –Susie

Dressing:

1 tablespoon	white balsamic vinegar
2 tablespoons	lemon juice (approx. 1 lemon)
½ teaspoon	honey
½ teaspoon	Dijon mustard
2 tablespoons	extra virgin olive oil

Salad:

4 cups	arugula, coarsely chopped
1 cup	fresh flat-leaf parsley, coarsely chopped
½ cup	mint, torn
1	large cucumber (approx. 2 cups), peeled & ½-inch diced
2	stalks celery, thinly sliced
1	red pepper, seeded & diced
2 cups	cherry or grape tomatoes, halved
1	(15.5 ounce) can chickpeas, drained & rinsed
	Sea salt & freshly ground black pepper

In a large salad bowl, whisk vinegar, lemon juice, honey, and mustard together. Slowly add olive oil until combined.

Place chopped arugula, parsley, and mint in salad bowl. *Do not toss with dressing until ready to serve.* Top the salad with cucumber, celery, red pepper, tomatoes, and chickpeas.

Salad can be refrigerated for up to an hour. When ready to serve, toss and season to taste with salt and pepper.

Note: This tangy salad is perfect with grilled meat!

Arugula 101: Lettuce or Herb?

Arugula is an herb often mistaken for lettuce and is known by a variety of names across the world. The English call it Rocket, while the French call it *Roquette*. A native of the Mediterranean land, arugula is very perishable and should be wrapped tightly for storage. For this recipe, select baby arugula, as the larger-leafed versions tend to be more bitter. If the herb is too strong for your palate, you can substitute or mix in rough chopped spinach as an alternative.

Chocolate Truffles

Serves 10, Yields 30

These dark chocolate truffles are the perfect 'dolce', or 'sweet ending' after a long and lingering Italian dinner. Serve with frozen grapes as a refreshing surprise. Oh, the sweet life! –Susie

⅔ cup	heavy cream
4 tablespoons	unsalted butter, softened
16 ounces	bittersweet chocolate, chopped
½ cup	cocoa powder
1 ½ cups	raw pistachios, almonds, walnuts or pecans, finely chopped
	Red grapes, washed & frozen

Bring cream to a boil over medium heat in a heavy saucepan, stirring constantly to make sure the cream does not scorch. Cook until the cream is reduced to ¼ cup. Remove from heat and add butter and chocolate. Allow ingredients to sit for a minute, and stir until smooth. If chocolate is not melted, place pan over very low heat, and stir to blend completely. Pour chocolate onto a large rimmed baking sheet, and spread with a spatula. Cover and place baking sheet in refrigerator for 1 hour.

Remove chocolate from refrigerator. Using a melon scoop or spoon, dip it in a small bowl of warm water, and scrape enough chocolate to gently shape a 1-inch ball. Be careful not to form the chocolate into a solid ball. Place on baking sheet lined with wax paper. Repeat this process to make approximately 30 balls. If the chocolate is not curling, it may be too cold or too hot.

Chill truffles in refrigerator for 30 minutes.

When ready to serve, remove chocolate truffles from the refrigerator and allow to rest for a few minutes. Place cocoa powder and chopped nuts in separate bowls. Roll each truffle through the cocoa, then the nuts. The truffles do not have to be perfectly round. Be careful not to compress the chocolate into a solid hard ball.

Note: Uncoated truffles can be kept in refrigerator for up to a week if placed in an airtight container and layered between sheets of wax paper.

From the Curious Cook...
In a Pinch for Time?

A friend fondly recalls one night when I brought out a pretty box of chocolates and ceremoniously untied the beautiful gold ribbon. The adults and teenagers alike had more fun passing the box and everyone carefully deciding which piece they would select. There was a lot of laughter and indecision... some plunged right in, while others wanted to rethink their choice... and now that some of these kids are leaving for college, we hope these dinners we've shared will fill them with happy stories from home to tell. –Susie

Limoncello

Flavorful imported *Limoncello*, an authentic lemon liqueur, is not expensive and can be easily found at most liquor stores. Keep *Limoncello* in the freezer and serve it cold, in a small glass prior to dessert. The tart sip of flavor is perfect alone or prior to indulging in sweets, such as these chocolate truffles.

tailgating traditions

The next generation continues the game day legacy

The next generation continues...

Our family bleeds garnet and gold, with the legacy of Florida State University calling many of us to the beautiful, red-bricked campus. Milton and I are both alumni; my sister, brother and assorted nieces graduated from FSU and our oldest daughter, Kyle, and niece, Logan, are currently enrolled at the university. With the spirit of true Southerners, game day tailgates are an integral part of fall traditions in our hometown.

Also Seminole alumni, Susie and Ed host a much-anticipated party at their home each year to stay in touch with old friends. Midway through football season sometimes as many as 250 friends gather on a Friday evening... partaking in fabulous foods and catching up with college buddies.

" Dadgummit! "
-Bobby Bowden

Growing up in Tallahassee, Milton nor Ed ever missed a home game and in the building years of the FSU football dynasty, when attendance was spotty, they could sit wherever they chose in the stadium. Great seats are much more difficult to score these days. Whether they are on their typical winning streak or a rare losing pattern, the men, like all good Seminoles, frequently reminisce about the many great plays - and those depressing "wide rights" - they have experienced from the sidelines.

As seasons have come and gone, tailgating has always been a part of our gameday celebrations. Yes, all of our girls wore the tiny FSU cheerleading costumes when they were tots. It is with great pride that we pass the "flaming spear" of delicious {and stylish} FSU tailgates along to the next generation... and we still happily partake in the traditions, enjoying great atmosphere and fabulous food before the Seminoles take the field.

Taylor, Logan and Courtney, 1996

Tailgating with Style

Clever ideas beyond boxed chicken and plastic tablecloths...

Adding a bit of pizazz to your tailgate traditions is simple and makes for memorable events to which your fan friends {and likely out-of-town rivals as well} will want to return for every game. Add personality to your party with a few small steps:

- Create small pennants in your team colors to add cheer to any tailgate spread - print, cut and tape to toothpicks for a bit of flair on otherwise average fruit and sandwich spreads.

- Don't skip the cloth tablecloth... it is the most simple way to add polish to your game day soirée. Head to the fabric store to select a fun pattern in your school's colors.

- Small flower arrangements in unusual containers will certainly add a bit of class to your pre-game festivities.

- Nothing shows your spirit like a signature drink to serve your guests. Pick your favorite beverage to serve and give it a rival name. This is guaranteed to add conversation to your party.

- Use footballs as part of your decoration. They may prompt a friendly game of catch.

Unconquered

Perhaps the most recognizable tradition in all of college football occurs in Doak Campbell Stadium at the beginning of every home game. A student portraying the famous Seminole Indian leader, Osceola, charges down the field on horseback in authentic regalia designed by the women of the Seminole tribe of Florida. The pinnacle of the tradition is when the dappled appaloosa horse, named Renegade, rears up on his back legs and Osceola plants a flaming spear on the 50-yard line. Go Noles!

menu

Oyster Shooters

Popcorn Balls

Cuban Sandwiches
with Tomato Jam

Browned Butter Brownies

Oyster Shooters

Serves 12, Yields 24

This is an easy and different way to serve oysters at a tailgate. Lucky for us, Tallahassee is located only 76 miles from the Apalachicola Bay, home of the most famous oyster beds. We have easy access to some of the best and freshest oysters in the world. –Susie

1 ½ cups	clamato juice or 1 cup tomato juice & ½ cup bottled clam juice
¼ cup	ketchup
¼ cup	fresh lime juice (approx. 2 limes)
1 teaspoon	hot sauce
¼ cup	sweet onion or green onions, finely chopped
¼ cup	fresh cilantro leaves, finely chopped (optional)
	Salt & pepper
½ cup	vodka, divided (optional)
24	raw oysters
	Saltine crackers
	Shot glasses

In a 5-cup container with a tight fitting lid, combine clamato juice, ketchup, lime juice, hot sauce, onion, and cilantro. Put on lid and shake until combined. Season to taste with salt and pepper, and additional hot sauce, if desired. If using vodka, start by adding ¼ cup to tomato mixture. Taste and add more vodka, if desired.

Place one oyster in each shot glass, and top with several teaspoons of tomato juice mixture. Serve immediately with saltine crackers on the side.

Hint: Plastic shot glasses can usually be found in most grocery stores near the straws, toothpicks, and other party items.

Get Shucking!

It is common at Florida State tailgates to find fans with bushels of oysters packed on ice for the day's festivities. Oysters can be enjoyed in a variety of ways, many of which are easy enough to serve from the back of a truck and are guaranteed to please a crowd. Serve them straight out of the shell, or perhaps, on a cracker with cocktail or hot sauce. For those who prefer them to be cooked, simply toss the entire shell on a hot grill and wait for the shell to slightly ease open, then pop off the top and enjoy. Or you can serve our Oyster Shooter Recipe... an easy way to spice up the party.

Popcorn Balls

Yields 8

These popcorn balls are fun to make and even more fun to eat... they are guaranteed to make you happy and may even bring out the kid in you! –Susie

3 bags	original microwave popcorn (approx. 15 cups), popped
1 cup	brown sugar
1 cup	light corn syrup
8 tablespoons	(2 sticks) butter
½ cup	water
1 teaspoon	salt
1 cup	dry roasted peanuts

Grease two large rimmed baking sheets. Place popped popcorn on one baking sheet and divide into eighths.

In a large saucepan, combine sugar, corn syrup, butter and water. Over medium-high heat, cook sugar mixture for 25 minutes or until it reaches 295 degrees, stirring continuously with a long wood spoon. Stir in salt and peanuts. Remove from heat.

Using rubber gloves, carefully pour syrup evenly over popcorn and quickly form popcorn into 8 balls. Place popcorn balls on other greased baking sheet and allow to cool. The popcorn balls can be stored in an airtight container for up to 4 days.

Hint: Popcorn balls are fun to make, but you have to be quick and it may take some practice. A candy thermometer and rubber gloves are a must!

From the Curious Cook... Rah Rah!

When I was little, my family would road trip to FSU football games a few times each season. My mom dressed me up and I happily wore my little cheerleading uniform. Sounds cute, but unfortunately it wasn't FSU garnet and gold... it was our local high school color - purple! My mom would fry chicken or quail, and pack cole slaw and three-bean salad... setting it all up on the camp table. It was well before the days of reserved Booster parking, so part of the adventure was finding the best lot, for the best price of course! Let's Go Seminoles! –Susie

Cuban Sandwiches with Tomato Jam

Serves 8

This Cuban sandwich is slightly unusual because unlike traditional recipes, we use pork tenderloin and add tomato jam. We were surprised in Dallas when we served them to locals who had never heard of and certainly had never eaten a Cuban. These sandwiches are such a staple in our Florida lives... it's amazing to realize how many people are missing out. I think we have converted our Bar-B-Que loving friends. –Susie

16-18 ounces	pork tenderloin
2	garlic cloves, sliced lengthwise into 6 slivers each
2 teaspoons	olive oil
1 teaspoon	ground coriander
1 teaspoon	ground cumin
1 teaspoon	fennel seeds
1 teaspoon	kosher salt
½ teaspoon	paprika
½ teaspoon	coarsely ground black pepper
¼ cup	mayonnaise
¼ cup	Dijon mustard
2	garlic cloves, mashed into paste
2	ciabatta loaves
½ pound	Serrano or Black Forest ham
½ pound	baby Swiss cheese
4	whole half-sour pickles, sliced thin lengthwise
¼ cup	pickled jalapeno slices
	Tomato Jam (see page 101)

Preheat oven to 350 degrees and adjust oven rack to the middle position.

Remove the silver membrane from the tenderloins. Using a small paring knife, cut slits in tenderloins and stuff with slivers of garlic. Place tenderloins in a medium roasting pan and drizzle with olive oil. Place spices in mortar and grind with pestle. Rub tenderloins with spice mixture, and return meat to roasting pan.

Place roasting pan in oven, and bake uncovered 30 minutes or until internal temperature of the meat reaches 150 degrees or cooked to desired doneness. Remember, meat will keep cooking once removed from oven.

Pre-Game Preparations

For tailgating, assemble these sandwiches at home, wrap in foil and store in an airtight container in your cooler. They'll be ready to throw on the grill and will certainly impress your crowd.

98

Allow tenderloin to rest for 10 minutes before slicing into 32 pieces. The pork can be made ahead and refrigerated until ready to prepare sandwiches.

To prepare sandwiches:
Prepare and light the grill.

Slice bread open face, and cut each loaf into 4 equal pieces. In small bowl, mix mayonnaise, mustard, and garlic paste. Spread mayonnaise mixture on cut sides of bread allowing 1 tablespoon per sandwich. Arrange pork, ham, cheese, pickles, jalapenos, to make 8 individual sandwiches. Top each sandwich with 2 tablespoons of Tomato Jam. Wrap each sandwich in foil. Grill and press until sandwich is warm and cheese is melted. Serve with store bought plantain chips.

Hint: Wrap several bricks in foil, and use them as weights to gently press the individual sandwiches.

Tomato Jam

Yields 1 cup

This jam adds just the right spice to Cuban sandwiches and is especially good served with blue cheese and crackers and a big glass of wine.   –Susie

1	(14.5 ounce) can diced tomatoes
1	small onion (½ cup), diced
¼ cup	apple cider vinegar
¼ cup	sugar
2 tablespoons	golden raisins (optional)
1 teaspoon	mustard seeds
⅛ teaspoon	ground cloves
⅛ teaspoon	nutmeg
¼ teaspoon	cinnamon
¼ teaspoon	curry powder (optional)
¼ teaspoon	cayenne pepper
	Salt

In a medium saucepan, combine tomatoes with onion, vinegar, sugar, and raisins. Stir in mustard seeds, ground cloves, nutmeg, cinnamon, curry, cayenne pepper, and a pinch of salt. Bring to a boil and then reduce heat to medium-low, stirring occasionally. Simmer for 45 minutes or until mixture is thick and jam like. Allow to cool and transfer to sterilized resealable container.

Note: Jam will keep for up to one month refrigerated.

Browned Butter Brownies

Yields 18

The browned butter adds a new depth of flavor to a traditional chocolate treat. These brownies are decadently rich, chewy delights that are a simple-to-prepare, fan favorite. – Susie

	Non-stick cooking spray with flour
20 tablespoons	(2 ½ sticks) unsalted butter
2 ½ cups	sugar
1 ½ cups	natural unsweetened cocoa
½ teaspoon	salt
1 tablespoon	water
2 teaspoons	vanilla extract
4	eggs
1 cup	all-purpose flour
1 ½ cups	Macadamia nuts, chopped (optional)

Preheat oven to 350 degrees and adjust oven rack to middle position.

Prepare a 9 x 13-inch baking dish with non-stick cooking spray with flour.

Melt butter in a medium saucepan over medium-high heat. While stirring constantly, continue to cook butter for 5 minutes or until brown bits start to form in bottom of saucepan, being careful not to burn the butter. Remove from heat and quickly stir in sugar, cocoa, salt, water, and vanilla. Transfer the hot chocolate mixture to a large mixing bowl. Allow chocolate to cool for 4 minutes.

Set mixer on medium-high and add eggs to hot chocolate mixture one at a time. Beat until blended after addition of each egg. Reduce mixer speed to low and gradually add flour. Mix until almost combined.

Using a spatula, fold in nuts and stir until blended. Pour batter into prepared pan. Bake in the center of oven for 35-40 minutes or until a skewer inserted in center comes out clean. Cool in pan; then turn out and cut into 18 equal pieces.

These can be made ahead and kept in an airtight container.

Will Work for Food

As the campus is situated just down the road from our design center, we have lots of Florida State University students, both past and present, employed by Coton Colors. We are lucky to have them as they are young, smart and full of energy. They have especially enjoyed this cookbook process... making great taste testers for recipes, especially these brownies!

Chili Cook-off on the Farm

Cooking up the flavors of fall amongst the Red Hills of South Georgia

Cooking up the flavors of fall...

Our hometown is perfectly situated so that the muggy summer days of North Florida fade into crisp fall afternoons spent among the rolling red hills and gracious oaks of South Georgia. While conveniently located just 30 miles from the coast, Tallahassee is also a short 20 miles {as the crow flies} from the Georgia border. We're fortunate that one of our long-time Coton Colors team members, Ashley, has a family farm nestled in the woods just over the state line. The change of the season beckons Southern-style celebrations, perfectly composed with the familiar twang of classic country tunes, relaxed chatter over favorite foods and evenings with bonfires blazing. These months happen to be the busiest for the Coton Colors team, yet each year we take an afternoon to just breathe the fresh air, gathering as a company to enjoy one another, express our gratitude for the hard work we've accomplished together and simply connect in

> "Thanksgiving, after all, is a word of action."
> —W.J. Cameron

a beautiful setting. Not quite a Thanksgiving feast, but a time to be thankful nonetheless. All of these people work tirelessly to make Coton Colors successful - many since the very early days of the company. They are the designers, thinkers and "do-ers" that make the magic happen and each possesses the heart and desire to bring the very best of themselves to work always. Although we spend each and every weekday {and lots of nights and weekends!} working closely together, it is always fun to take a break, change our scenery and relax spending time over a memorable meal together.

While the day is spent with a bit of competitive skeet shooting, early evening finds us gently swaying in the rockers on the old wooden front porch and dusk brings lots of laughter around the roaring fire... and most importantly, no one heads home on an empty stomach.

Harvesting Great Décor

Embrace the change of seasons with these clever fall design ideas

- Leave the leaves - Nothing says fall like leaves rustling beneath your feet... no need to 'clean up' the setting; instead just embrace the season. Keep a rake handy in case children want to make a big pile of leaves to jump in... again and again!

- Dot your pumpkins - These pretty pumpkins aren't painted, but instead are "polka dotted" with Coton Colors style. Simply use an apple corer to remove plugs from your pumpkin, then replace with plugs from various squash, fall gourds or different hued pumpkins.

- Scrap happy - Save your fabric scraps, you never know when you may be able to recycle them into table runners! We used left over ticking fabric to drape the food table with rustic style. Just simply cut to size using pinking shears for a no-sew finished look.

- Let the outdoor décor work for you - fall offers an abundance of decorating materials... use what's available! Feed corn, poured in a jar or bucket, makes a perfect base to support branches of cotton, helping you to create a fitting arrangement for any fall gathering.

menu

Chipotle Pecans

Pumpkin Seed Cornbread

Vegetarian Chili

"Second Place" Chili

Fresh Apple Cake
with Caramel Icing

Chipotle Pecans

Serves 12, Yields 8 cups

The pine-like essence of rosemary and the warm, smokey flavor of chipotle chili pepper combines with hints of maple syrup and orange juice to create the perfect sweet and savory snack! –Susie

2 tablespoons	olive oil
⅓ cup	100% pure maple syrup
¼ cup	light brown sugar
¼ cup	fresh squeezed orange juice (approx. ½ orange)
2 ½ teaspoons	chipotle powder
4-5 tablespoons	fresh rosemary leaves, minced & divided
1 tablespoon	kosher salt, divided
2 pounds	shelled pecans
	Vegetable oil

In a large bowl, mix olive oil, syrup, sugar, juice, chipotle powder, 2 tablespoons rosemary, and 2 teaspoons salt. Add pecans and toss. Set aside.

Preheat oven to 350 degrees and adjust oven rack to middle position. Grease a large rimmed baking sheet with vegetable oil.

Spread the pecans on baking sheet and toast for 30 minutes, stirring twice. Bake 5 minutes longer or until they are nicely toasted and fragrant. Remove from oven and sprinkle with remaining rosemary and salt.

Allow to cool and toss occasionally to prevent pecans from sticking together. Store in airtight container.

Rolling Red Hills

The Red Hills Region extends from just east of the Aucilla River to west of the Ochlockonee River, and from the farmlands near Coolidge, Georgia down to Tallahassee, Florida. The hills are "red" due to the red clay soil that covers the rolling hills, ravines and gullies of the area. At one time, plantations in Leon County, Florida were the 5th largest producers of cotton in all of Georgia and Florida. After the Civil War, the Red Hills plantations became destinations for quail hunters and rich northerners. The Red Hills Region also has the largest concentration of undeveloped plantation lands in the United States. This region has been identified by the Nature Conservancy who has designated the Red Hills as one of America's "Last Great Places."

Pumpkin Seed Cornbread

Serves 12-16

Years ago, I made this cornbread for a dinner party and my friend, Patty, asked me for the recipe. Since then, she has made a few changes, and I think the new version is far better than my original. The pumpkin seeds are a must! –Susie

	Non-stick cooking spray with flour
1 cup	cheddar cheese, shredded
½ cup	buttermilk
2	(10 ounce) packages frozen cream-style corn, thawed
2	(8.5 ounce) packages corn muffin mix
1	(4.5 ounce) can chopped green chiles, drained
1 ½ cups	sweet onion (approx. 2 medium), chopped
½ cup	sour cream
½ cup	unsalted pumpkin seeds (pepitas)

Preheat oven to 400 degrees and adjust oven rack to middle position.

Prepare one 9 x 13-inch, or two 8 x 8-inch, baking pans using non-stick cooking spray with flour.

In a large bowl, combine cheese, buttermilk, cream-style corn, corn muffin mix, chiles, onion, and sour cream. Stir until dry ingredients are moistened. Pour batter into prepared dish and sprinkle the top with pumpkin seeds. Bake for 20-30 minutes or until a toothpick inserted in center comes out clean.

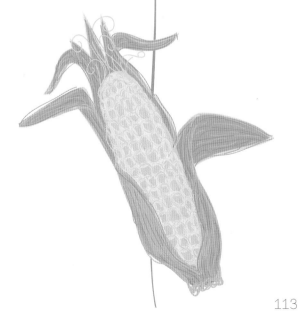

Vegetarian Chili

Serves 12

Although this is not a traditional style chili, once you try it, I promise, you will make it again and again. –Susie

Chili
Cook-off

Can you really call vegetarian chili, chili?? Since Susie has been an integral part of the Coton Colors team this year, it was fitting she join us for our annual company gathering, and why not add a little friendly competition to the mix? Susie brought her delicious Vegetarian Chili, while Laura ladled out her classic Meat Chili {recipe on following page}, and though most of the Coton Colors men frowned at the idea of meatless chili, it was the vegetarian variety that took the coveted title!

½ cup	olive oil
2	medium sweet onions, coarsely chopped
4	garlic cloves, minced
2	red peppers, cored & coarsely chopped
3	medium zucchini, cut ½-inch chunks
2 pounds	fresh plum tomatoes, seeded & coarsely chopped
2	(28 ounce) cans diced tomatoes
1	(15.5 ounce) can red kidney beans, drained & rinsed
1	(15.5 ounce) can chick peas, drained & rinsed
2 tablespoons	chili powder
1 tablespoon	dried basil
1 tablespoon	cumin
1 tablespoon	oregano
1 teaspoon	fennel seeds
1 teaspoon	salt
2 teaspoons	black pepper
1	lemon, halved
½ cup	fresh dill, chopped
½ cup	fresh flat-leaf parsley, chopped

For garnish:

½ cup	fresh dill, chopped
½ cup	fresh flat-leaf parsley, chopped
2 cups	sour cream
2 cups	cheese, shredded
1	bunch green onions, chopped

In a large pot, heat olive oil over medium-high heat. Add onions and cook for 7-10 minutes until they are translucent. Reduce heat to medium. Add garlic, red peppers, zucchini, and sauté 7-10 minutes until vegetables are just tender. *Do not overcook.* Stir in tomatoes and beans.

In a small bowl, combine chili powder, basil, cumin, oregano, fennel, salt and pepper. Pour spice mixture into palm of hand and rub hands together over pot of chili to release flavors or use a mortar and pestle to crush spices before adding them to chili.

Squeeze juice of one lemon into the pot and stir in fresh dill and parsley. Reduce heat to low and cook uncovered for 30-45 minutes only, stirring occasionally. This chili tastes best when the zucchini, tomatoes and beans are tender, but not mushy. It is important not to simmer the chili for a long period of time or overcook it. Turn off heat to let flavors blend and then reheat when ready to serve. Season to taste with salt and more chili powder, if needed.

Offer sour cream, shredded cheese, green onions, chopped dill and parsley as garnishes.

Note: Keep the chili powder shaker close by in case someone wants extra spice... Some people like hot sauce too!

"Second Place" Chili

Serves 6-8

I think Laura's meat chili is fantastic {I'll go so far as to say fabulous!} and you will too! –Susie

1 pound	ground beef
1	large onion, chopped
1	(35 ounce) can chopped tomatoes
1	(6 ounce) can tomato paste
1	(15 ounce) can spicy chili beans, mostly drained
3 tablespoons	chili powder
½ teaspoon	cayenne pepper
½ teaspoon	red pepper flakes
1 tablespoon	sugar
1 tablespoon	salt
1 teaspoon	black pepper

For garnish:

1 cup	sharp cheddar cheese, grated
1 cup	sour cream
	Saltine crackers

In large pot, sauté ground beef and onion over medium-high heat until beef is cooked through and onions are translucent. Drain off fat and return meat mixture to pot. Stir in tomatoes, tomato paste, and all seasonings {more chili powder if you like it spicy!}. Bring to a boil and reduce heat. Cover and simmer on low, stirring occasionally, for one hour. Stir in beans and continue cooking for 30 minutes longer. Taste and add more seasoning if needed The longer this sits, the better it is... even better the next day!

Serve with toppings of cheese and sour cream with a side of Saltine crackers for dipping.

Note: Always grate from the whole block of good quality cheddar for a fresher taste.

A day at the Farm...

I have been blessed over the years with the most amazing team of employees at Coton Colors. One in particular, Ashley, has worked with me for over a decade and has seen our company through many stages of growth. In the early days, Ashley began her Coton Colors career as "Dee's helper" in our busy {and often chaotic} pottery studio. Her talents were quickly recognized and she has patiently grown with us {consequently holding every job imaginable} along the way. She now serves in her current position as our Operations Manager.

We have celebrated many milestones together over the years, and I have enjoyed comparing parenting stories of raising her three boys to my three girls as they have grown through kindergarten, middle school and high school concurrently. We are lucky that Ashley is gracious enough to share her family's farm with us for employee gatherings. Here is why this place is so special to Ashley and now, to us too.

In Ashley's words...
As male turkeys are known as "Toms", my Father and five of his closest friends purchased "Six Toms Farm" 35 years ago. All six families have truly enjoyed gathering there with lifelong friends ever since. 'The Farm', as we affectionately call it, has always been a favorite place of mine. I'm sure my husband, Mark, considered gaining access to The Farm when marrying me a major plus, and now our three boys have practically been raised there.

Set amidst historically famous plantations, live oaks and longleaf pines, The Farm is tucked along a winding red clay dirt road. The simple "Six Toms" sign marks the entrance... and the men choose to display it out on the fence only when they want to be found {which isn't often!}.

During the fall, my husband and sons spend more time at The Farm than at home. They scour the fields for whatever game is in season - quail, duck, deer - and chase the river for catfish {which I am happy to enjoy fried, alongside onion rings, straight from the fryer}.

Thanksgiving is the one time each year that the wives and daughters actually get an open invitation to The Farm from the "Six Toms". Thanksgiving Eve finds all of the 'menfolk' {and the kids} at an annual camp-style sleepover - complete with a blazing fire, long walks to the outhouse and complaints of snoring. The next day, a crowd of nearly 100 family and friends ascend; the men "man their posts" as the turkeys cook in six fryers, while the women fuss over the antiquated oven set, warming up numerous covered dishes in the outdoor kitchen.

Though just outside of town and across the state line, the pace and charm of The Farm is just right... no deadlines to interrupt quality time amongst those friends and family that we love the most.

- ashley

Fresh Apple Cake with Caramel Icing

Serves 10-12

If you like caramel apples, you will love this recipe. It is quite possibly my favorite cake to eat because the combination of apples and caramel remind me of my favorite season, fall. It is simple to make because you don't use a mixer and you don't even have to preheat the oven. –Susie

Apple Cake:

	Non-stick baking spray with flour
1 ½ cups	vegetable oil
2 cups	sugar
3	eggs, beaten
3 cups	red delicious apples, peeled, cored, & coarsely chopped
1 cup	pecans, chopped
3 cups	all-purpose flour
1 teaspoon	salt
1 teaspoon	baking soda
2 teaspoons	vanilla extract

Icing:

8 tablespoons	(1 stick) butter
1 cup	light brown sugar, packed
¼ cup	evaporated milk
1 teaspoon	vanilla extract
	Pecans, for decoration

Prepare two, 9-inch round cake pans using non-stick baking spray with flour.

In a large bowl, combine by hand (*do not use a mixer*) oil, sugar, eggs, apples, and pecans; set aside. Sift flour, salt, and baking soda into a medium bowl. Repeat, sifting dry ingredients two additional times. Gradually add the dry ingredients to the apple mixture, and stir by hand until combined. Add vanilla and stir.

Pour an equal amount of batter into two 9-inch cake pans. Adjust rack to middle position and place both cake pans into cold oven. Set oven to 325 degrees. Bake for 45 minutes or until middle is set. Remove from oven and place on rack to cool.

Late Night Sweets... Give me 'Some-More'

For any event with a bonfire, always keep the fixins' for s'mores on hand. On a cool fall evening, many guests will linger a little longer, well after the meal {and dessert!}, to enjoy the fireside fellowship. Despite a hearty meal of perfect comfort foods, it seems as if there's always room for s'mores!

It is best to make the icing while cake is baking, or immediately after the cake is removed from oven.

In a small saucepan, combine butter and brown sugar over medium heat. Stir until butter is melted and sugar is dissolved. Add evaporated milk and bring to a boil. Remove pan from heat and stir in vanilla. Allow icing and cake layers to cool completely before assembling the cake. Half of the icing goes between the layers and half on top of the cake. {It is fine if some icing drips down the sides, in fact, it looks better!} Decorate top of cake with chopped or whole pecans.

Hint: This is a two layer cake recipe, but the recipe can easily be doubled. If making a four layer cake, push a bamboo skewer through the bottom three layers, to prevent sliding.

Bradley's Country Store...

The traditions of Tallahassee run deep, from its sprawling oaks to its pine-scented woods. A nostalgic drive along the moss-draped canopy roads takes you to another of its longheld traditions, to the simpler lifestyle of Bradley's Country Store... a common destination for Tallahasseans. Bradley's roots began in 1910, with Mary Bradley selling sausage from her kitchen window, and then continued with the storefront opening in 1927. Today, Mary's son, Mr. Bradley and his daughter Jan Bradley Parker, still cater to a diverse and loyal crowd all seeking a taste of the secret-ingredient sausage and freshly smoked meats.

The narrow wooden aisles of the quaint, tin-roofed store sell everything from Moon Pies and Yoo Hoos, to classic candies and country milled grits {for which the Bradley's are famed}. Making a visit to Bradley's is a step back in time for visiting customers. No purchase is complete without a fresh sausage dog and an ice-cold bottled Coca Cola... only to be enjoyed in a rocking chair on the store's front porch in the good company of local farmers in overalls and well-heeled ladies alike.

Tallahassee is fortunate to have Bradley's Country Store for fresh meats and smoked sausage, but most communities have a talented local butcher. It is wise to utilize them as they often give trusted advice and personal service.

Coton Colors Art Manager and Stylist, Paige, recalls her annual Christmas tradition at Bradley's Country Store.

In Paige's words...
During the hustle and bustle of the Christmas season, I typically find myself in overcrowded parking lots by day and various holiday gatherings by night, so I'm usually ready for a bit of solitude before the grand finale of the holiday festivities commence. On Christmas Eve, I always enjoy a visit to Bradley's to gather the last gifts on my list. The scenic drive - a treat in itself - is the perfect way for me to wind down and enjoy a simpler way of life. My purchase of fresh link sausage wrapped in white butcher paper is nearly a perfect gift... only lacking a simple red bow, so I always bring a spool of ribbon and scissors along. The rest of the afternoon is spent delivering the goodies to my friends and neighbors. It makes me happy to hear that most have made it their tradition to serve it on Christmas morning. The experience always satisfies my craving for simple traditions and an old fashioned Christmas.

- Paige

Tidings from a Christmas Kitchen

Turning busy preparations into memorable moments

Turning busy preparations...

Being an artist {who creates gifts and décor during the biggest gift giving time of the year} makes me a very busy girl around the holidays. This was especially true in the early days of Coton Colors when our small team was hand-painting and personalizing every single piece of pottery that the company shipped. I can recall a time when my daughters and nieces were younger and their Christmas breaks from school were spent painting and packing our custom ornaments. We laugh together about how we gave each of the six cousins a "quota" to meet {and yes, of course we paid them... a little}. The baby, Mary Parker, wanted nothing more than to move up from 'packer' to 'painter,' and the girls quickly figured out how to create assembly lines to get the job done faster so that they could go out to enjoy the day. I think that they looked forward to the day school started back, but

"Gifts of time and love are surely the basic ingredients of a truly Merry Christmas."

-Peg Bracken

they definitely thank us now for inspiring their individual creativity and teaching them how to work hard. It was character building, right?

Even though today we have production houses to help with the hand-painting {and I try hard not to stress as much through the season}, I still find myself exhausted as Christmas Day arrives. I am eternally grateful that Milton is a huge lover of holidays, especially all things Christmas. His child-like excitement for the holiday has always ensured that we enjoy the season - from the selecting and decorating of the tree to the thoughtfully-chosen gifts beneath it. And thanks to his enthusiasm and demand that we all stay "on task", by the time the day arrives we are able to relax for a brief moment, basking in the company of our family.

Now that the girls are older, I no longer "force" them to paint during the holidays {although they often choose to work at the Coton Colors design center during the season}. We do our best to carve out a bit of quality time together, giddy with the joy and anticipation of Christmas. We've encouraged the girls to find their own artistry and creativity, and it certainly shines in the gifts they select for Christmas. I've also learned to "challenge" them in recent years to contribute their own tastes to Christmas, which sometimes leads to laughter as we try out the recipes of their choosing. In the moments just before the 25th, as the professional demands finally slow, we join forces in the kitchen, creating delicious foods and thoughtful gifts at the same time. We relish in accomplishing two necessary holiday tasks in tandem... and having a bit of fun too!

These times together at home, crafting and creating gifts, call for simple meals that can be enjoyed while working away. Susie's holiday menu is full of comfort foods just perfect for cold nights spent prepping presents for loved ones. You can't go wrong with a warm cup of Tomato Soup paired with a yummy sandwich. Plus, serving soup in a mug allows for sipping between stuffing stockings and trimming trees. Although most of the holiday is focused appropriately on Christmas morning, times gathered with your family leading up to that special day can truly bring out the real joy of the season.

Happy Everything

MERRY CHRISTMAS

love, the johnsons

menu

Classic Holiday Stuffed Celery

Homemade Tomato Soup

Creamy Potato Soup

Prosciutto, Pear & Blue
Cheese Sandwich
with Fig Jam

Buttery Poundcake
with Nutella Swirl

Sugared Ginger Cookies

Classic Holiday Stuffed Celery

Serves 6-8, Yields 18

My grandmother and her sister, Mary loved this appetizer. They would make it for every holiday and served it with jumbo black olives as a side dish. My aunt still makes platters of this Stuffed Celery at our family gatherings, and we all laugh and remember our grandmothers and their love of food and family. —Susie

8 ounces	cream cheese
¾ cup	pimento stuffed green Spanish olives, chopped
2 tablespoons	olive juice
6	stalks celery, ends trimmed
	Paprika, to garnish

In a small bowl, put cream cheese, olives and olive juice. Mix with a fork until blended; add more juice if needed. Spoon cream cheese mixture into a small resealable plastic bag and refrigerate until ready to serve. Simply snip one corner of the bag and pipe cream cheese into celery stalks. Cut each piece of stuffed celery into 3 equal pieces and place on platter. Sprinkle with paprika.

From the Curious Cook...
A Love of Food

My Grandmother always told the story of how my Great Grandfather {a Presbyterian preacher} would ask early in the day what was being served for Sunday supper. He would then talk about the anticipated meal all day long, so that everyone's appetites would be thoroughly "lathered up", well before mealtime. His hankering for the awaited meal was contagious and inherently resulted in a full table come supper time... his ultimate goal. He adored my Great Grandmother {and her cooking} and told her so often. —Susie

Homemade Tomato Soup

Serves 4-6, Yields 8 Cups

I recently started using a new technique that has changed the way I make things that call for a fresh tomato base. To replace the labor intensive method of blanching and peeling tomatoes, I've learned to use a simple box cheese grater to grate the tomato, which easily separates the flesh from the skin. Don't forget to remove the tomato seeds prior to grating, as the seeds have the tendency to add bitterness to your sauce or soup. Over-ripe tomatoes are ideal to use with this technique. –Susie

4 pounds	very ripe tomatoes
2 tablespoons	olive oil
1 cup	sweet onion, chopped
3	garlic cloves, minced
2 tablespoons	tomato paste
2 tablespoons	all-purpose flour
2 cups	vegetable broth
1 teaspoon	sugar
1 teaspoon	salt
½ teaspoon	coarsely ground black pepper
2 tablespoons	fresh basil, chopped
½ cup	heavy cream
½	lemon, juiced
	Salt & black pepper
6	small basil leaves, to garnish

Cut tomatoes in half horizontally and use finger to remove the seeds. Using a box grater, grate tomato pulp into large bowl and discard the tomato skins. Set grated tomato pulp aside.

Place 2 tablespoons of olive oil in a large sauce pan and heat oil over medium heat. Add onions and sauté for 3 minutes. Add garlic to pan and cook for 2 minutes longer. Stir in tomatoes and tomato paste and continue to cook for 2-3 minutes. Sprinkle flour over tomato mixture and stir until combined. Add vegetable broth, sugar, salt and pepper, and bring soup to a simmer while stirring. Cook for 10 minutes or until the soup begins to thicken. Remove from heat, stir in chopped basil, and set aside to allow soup to cool.

Pour cooled soup in blender and process until smooth. Return soup to the same pan and add cream. Over medium heat, stir and bring soup to a simmer. Stir in lemon juice. Season to taste with salt and pepper. Ladle soup into bowls and garnish with basil leaves.

Creamy Potato Soup

Serves 4-6, Yields 8 cups

This potato soup is my mom's recipe and a favorite of my dad's. As a child, I remember that she would make this for my brother & me when we had a cold or didn't feel up to par. Comforting... thanks, Mom! –Susie

2 pounds	potatoes (approx. 4), peeled & thinly sliced
3 cups	water
1 teaspoon	salt
2 cups	milk
2 tablespoons	butter
⅔ cup	green onions (approx. 4), chopped
⅓ cup	parsley, chopped
½ teaspoon	white pepper
½	lemon
	Salt & coarsely ground black pepper, to taste

In a large pot, combine potatoes and 3 cups of water; bring to a boil over high heat. Add 1 teaspoon salt and reduce heat to medium-high. Cover and cook 10 minutes or until potatoes are tender. Do not drain the water. Let cool slightly. Mash potatoes until lumpy. Take a good pinch of the green onions and parsley, set aside for garnish.

Stir in milk, butter, green onions, parsley, and white pepper and bring to a simmer over medium-high heat. A squeeze of lemon will brighten the flavors. Season to taste with salt and black pepper.

Ladle into bowls, garnish with green onions and parsley. Serve and enjoy!

Merry Christmas!

A Gift of Comfort

Soups can be thoughtful, unexpected gifts during the holidays or anytime for friends under the weather. Large mason jars with custom, hand-created tags make for perfect presentation and recipients are certainly grateful for the meals-on-wheels delivery!

Prosciutto, Pear & Blue Cheese Sandwiches with Fig Jam

Serves 4

Sliced Italian fontina, shaved Manchego or Pecorino Romano cheese would work nicely too. It's the holiday season... have fun! This gourmet sandwich is a festive mix of tastes and traditions and is the perfect companion to homemade soup. *–Susie*

8	thick slices multi grain bread
2 tablespoons	soft butter
1 tablespoon	olive oil
2 teaspoons	balsamic vinegar
1 teaspoon	honey
2 cups	arugula leaves
2 teaspoons	Dijon mustard (optional)
⅛ teaspoon	coarsely ground black pepper
2 ounces	prosciutto, thinly sliced
1	pear, cored & thinly sliced
2 ounces	blue cheese, sliced
	Fig Jam (see page 138)

Adjust oven rack to second position from the top and preheat broiler to low.

Place slices of bread on baking sheet. Broil until lightly toasted. Turn bread over and butter untoasted sides of all 8 slices. Continue to broil a few minutes until golden. Remove from oven.

In a bowl, blend olive oil, balsamic vinegar, honey, and toss with arugula.

Take 4 slices of bread, butter side up, and spread with Dijon mustard. Top with the arugula and sprinkle with pepper. Next, evenly distribute the prosciutto, pear, and blue cheese. Finally, spread the butter side of the remaining slices of toasted bread with Fig Jam and place jam side down to complete the sandwich.

Note: Baby spinach can be used as a substitute for arugula.

Fig Jam

Yields 1 cup

This Fig Jam is wonderful on sandwiches or served with Brie and crackers, as a nice addition to a winter cheese board. —Susie

1 cup	water
4 ounces	dried figs
3 tablespoons	olive oil
1 cup	red onion (1 small), diced
1 teaspoon	ground cinnamon
½ teaspoon	ground nutmeg
¼ teaspoon	ground cumin
¼ teaspoon	cayenne pepper
½ teaspoon	salt
¼ teaspoon	black pepper
¼ cup	apple cider vinegar
⅓ cup	sugar
1	lemon, zested & juiced
	Salt & black pepper, to taste

In a small saucepan, bring 1 cup of water to boil. Add dried figs to pan and remove from heat. Allow figs to soften for 15 minutes. Using slotted spoon, remove figs from liquid and place on cutting board to cool. Set fig liquid aside.

Pour olive oil in a large skillet and sauté onion for 5 minutes over medium heat. Place seasonings and salt and pepper in mortar and grind with pestle before adding to onion mixture. Remove stems from figs, chop, and add to pan. Add fig liquid, vinegar, sugar, and lemon juice. Stir and simmer over medium-low heat for 30 minutes or until the mixture is sticky and jam like.

Remove from heat and stir in lemon zest. Season to taste with salt and pepper, and add more cayenne pepper, if desired. Allow to cool.

Note: Jam will keep for several weeks refrigerated.

Buttery Pound Cake
with Nutella Swirl

Serves 8

My daughter, Kate, loves the chocolate and hazelnut spread - Nutella. This simple, marbled pound cake is one of her favorites. We always look forward to saving some for breakfast to go alongside a strong cup of coffee.   –Susie

	Non-stick baking spray with flour
4	eggs, room temperature
2 teaspoons	pure vanilla extract
1 ½ cups	all-purpose flour
¾ teaspoon	baking powder
¼ teaspoon	salt
12 tablespoons	(1 ½ sticks) unsalted butter, softened
1 ⅓ cups	sugar
1 cup	Nutella
1 tablespoon	unsweetened natural cocoa

Preheat oven to 325 degrees and adjust oven rack to the middle position. Prepare loaf pan with non-stick baking spray with flour.

In a small bowl, whisk eggs with vanilla and set aside. Sift flour, baking powder, and salt into medium bowl and set aside. Place butter and sugar in a large mixing bowl. Using an electric mixer, beat softened butter and sugar until blended. Reduce mixer speed to low and gradually add whisked eggs. Increase mixer speed and beat until creamy. Add flour mixture a little at a time and mix until just combined.

Pour ½ cup of cake batter into a medium bowl, add Nutella and cocoa, stir until combined. Chocolate will look like thick brownie batter.

Pour ⅓ of the cake batter into the prepared loaf pan. Crumble half the chocolate mixture on top of cake batter in loaf pan. Repeat with ⅓ batter and the remaining chocolate. Swirl batter and chocolate with a wooden skewer, but do not over mix. Top with remaining batter.

Place in oven, and bake for 1 hour 15 minutes or until toothpick inserted in center of cake comes out clean.

Turn oven off and allow cake to sit in oven for an additional 5 minutes. Remove from oven and place on rack to cool for at least 30 minutes. Remove cake from pan and allow it to cool right side up on rack for 1 ½ hours before serving.

Sugared Ginger Cookies

Yields approximately 60 cookies

These ginger cookies are unlike any that you've have ever tasted. They have just the right amount of sweetness. This recipe comes from the mother of Coton Colors Art Manager and Stylist, Paige... and I must say, they are perfect and will become a new tradition for The Murray's this Christmas. —Susie

2 cups	all-purpose flour, divided
4 tablespoons	all-purpose flour, divided
1 teaspoon	baking soda
1 ½ teaspoons	ground ginger
1 teaspoon	ground cinnamon
½ teaspoon	ground cloves
1 cup	light brown sugar, packed
12 tablespoons	(1 ½ sticks) unsalted butter, melted
¼ cup	unsulfured molasses
1	egg
¼ cup	granulated sugar

Preheat oven to 350 degrees. Line baking sheet with parchment paper.

Sift together 1 cup and 2 tablespoons of flour, baking soda, ginger, cinnamon, and cloves into a large mixing bowl. Stir in brown sugar. Whisk in melted butter, molasses and egg. Stir in an additional 1 cup and 2 tablespoons of flour. Cover the dough and chill for at least 1 hour, or up to two days.

Pour granulated sugar in small bowl. When ready to bake cookies, scoop a tablespoon of dough and shape into a ball. Roll each ball in granulated sugar. Place 2 inches apart on the prepared baking sheet lined with parchment paper. Bake for 10-12 minutes. Cool on wire rack.

Christmas Tree

Milton's very favorite holiday decoration is the Christmas tree. It is a tradition every year to gather his girls and head out to choose the tree. He is picky, really picky. Once, Milton actually returned a tree after he got it home because it just wasn't right. Really. He brought it home, put it in the stand, strung the lights, began decorating it, then decided it was too small... and returned it! Milton's love for this holiday is endearing, and you can bet the chosen tree is always a beautiful sight to behold!

143

Chinese New Year's Eve

Ringing in the New Year with Asian inspired flair

Ringing in the New Year...

The idea of twisting a bit of Asian flair into the time-honored, traditional New Year's Eve gathering came to me shortly after returning from my travels to China, as we prepared to ring in 2011 with friends. I travel to Asia several times a year and I love to share the many stories and customs I encounter with my friends when I arrive back home. It's an amazing culture full of rich traditions and it never ceases to surprise me. Chinese New Year is a BIG deal in China with over-the-top rituals and decorations, however, the basic meaning of New Year celebrations transcends the globe. The traditions of the Chinese New Year are very similar to those that we recognize in the U.S. - to reconcile, forget all grudges and sincerely wish peace and happiness for everyone.

For our 2011 Chinese New Year's celebration, we married the customs and dishes of our culture with those from China, creating a fun evening with a twist. In China, providing a meal to friends, family and colleagues is considered the ultimate compliment and the time spent together is an excellent way to build *Guanxi*, or 'positive relationships' between people. Susie definitely succeeded in culinary *Guanxi* with her memorable menu fused with flavorful sauces and spices.

The décor for the evening was inspired by the Asian markets I frequent during my travels. From the antique Chinese lanterns and handmade origami, to the painted chopsticks and dragon plates, we created the perfect atmosphere with little effort. We hoped that the splash of Asian touches would promise a 'fate of good fortune and wealth' for all in the year to come. We even tied in a few of their most unique rituals, like the graceful lighting of wish lanterns that my sister, Marcie, and I first experienced in Thailand. It created a truly unforgettable evening marking gratitude for all our many blessings and fortuity for the years to come.

> **"Be not afraid of growing slowly, be afraid only of standing still."**
>
> -Chinese Proverb

Creative Culture

Clever tips to easily achieve an Asian inspired atmosphere

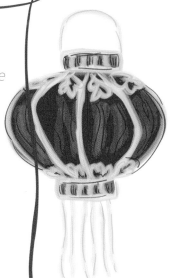

○ We were lucky to find beautiful old lanterns at a local antique market but we have found that many stores carry paper lanterns in lots of different colors. Buy them by the dozen and hang these over your table to add an authentic touch to your party.

○ An easy, low-cost display of clocks from around your home will make a unique statement on a mantle and your guests will enjoy watching the time tick to midnight. Or, set each one to a particular time zone and have fun celebrating as each region rings in its own New Year.

○ Inexpensive dry white rice in a simple, decorative bowl makes a well-themed display of chopsticks for the meal. Buy a variety of chopsticks in multiple colors so that each guest can keep track of them throughout the party.

○ Chinese takeout boxes make an easy container for a burst of blooms. Simply line the inside of the box with foil to hold the moisture from the oasis and arrange away using an assortment of flowers. These arrangements are big enough to make a statement, but small enough to be used in many places. Place them throughout your home individually or in clusters, on the bar, the buffet, in the powder room, or foyer, to create décor continuity for your event. Guests will be thrilled to take these home as party favors. Don't forget the chopsticks! These can be found at local Asian Markets, or you could purchase some from your favorite Chinese restaurant.

Red Lanterns

Signifying fortune and wealth, red lanterns are hung during Chinese New Year to attract good luck in the coming year. We have several hanging in our Tallahassee studio as a symbol of bright happiness in hopes of a prosperous future.

Lighting the night...

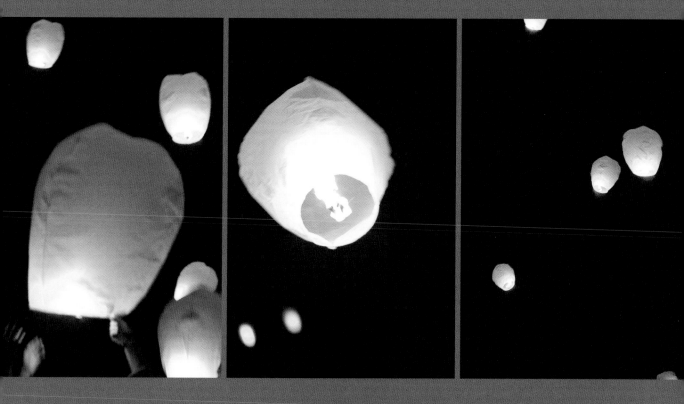

An Asian-themed New Year's event provides the perfect opportunity to create a tradition far exceeding the expectation of fireworks. We incorporated breathtaking Sky Lanterns {or *Kongming Lanterns*} into our own event and our guests are still talking about the display of light, luck and love we created. I first experienced this beautiful tradition, which is symbolic of destiny and prosperity, during my travels to Thailand. The releasing of Sky Lanterns began in Old Asia as a way to whisk away troubles into the fresh air and they are often used in Far Eastern weddings and celebrations to send wishes and prayers closer to the heavens. For our celebration, each guest wrote his or her wish on the lantern, lit it and sent it into the sky for a beautiful display of New Year's resolutions.

Chinese Food
Fresh and Always Delicious

For many years, Coton Colors products were all handmade in our Florida studios. With our fortunate growth, we made the leap a few years ago to manufacture overseas, which has allowed us to focus our studio efforts on design. This has given me the opportunity to travel to Asia several times annually to visit our overseas factories and business associates, keeping a close watch on the production of our handcrafted products. I am fortunate to have my sister, Marcie, join me on each venture and long time Coton Colors employees, Meghan and Paige frequently share in our adventures. Our travels have immersed us in the traditions of this intriguing society. Paul, who serves as our sourcing agent in China and whom I respect as a dear friend, has taught us to stretch our palates far beyond American-style Chinese food. He has provided us countless opportunities to learn the complexities of the Chinese culture. Here are some of the dishes and dining experiences we have enjoyed during our visits.

- Laura

Authentic Chinese Dining

As restaurants are always very busy, dirty dishes from the previous diners are whisked away and tables are set with a clean white tablecloth once new guests are seated. Each diner receives a small saucer into which soy sauce is poured, a small wooden plate holding a hot, steaming towel {your washcloth, which is a necessity}, a teacup {no handle as you don't need to drink if it is too hot to hold} with saucer and chopsticks with a rest so as not to dirty the tablecloth. Also included is another set of black chopsticks used for serving, a small bowl and "spoon" into which many different side dishes are served. Last but not least, there is always a wrapped toothpick for use during or after your meal.

No matter the hour of the day {or night}, restaurants are always brightly lit and bustling with energy. There is lots of hustle and bustle, with dishes constantly clanking and the sound of tea pouring from teapots... clang-clang-clang. We are always, always seated at a round table with a giant lazy susan in the center. My daughter, Mary Parker, loves this idea as she is often the one caught in the middle passing dishes back and forth and her only request during our recent kitchen renovation was to add one to our family table.

Steamed Fish

With the Guangdong province sitting on China's Southern coast, fresh seafood is a specialty of Cantonese cuisine. Many authentic restaurants we visit, especially while in Hong Kong, maintain live seafood tanks with all types of sealife swimming {some of the most unexpected meals can be experienced at these local seafood markets}. The tip is to have someone like 'a Paul' with you to handle the 30-minute {or longer} event of dinner selection, which includes placing flopping fish on the ground to determine freshness by the speed with which they "swim". Once a fish has adequately danced its way to Paul's liking and the negotiation of purchase has been settled, we shuffle through the slippery stall to a perfectly nice restaurant tucked behind, where the fish that was begging to be chosen moments before is now steamed for our pleasure. The Chinese truly take great pride in fresh fare!

Peking Duck

Of all of the delicious dishes we eat in China, the one both Marcie and I love the most is this famous food from Bejiing, prepared since the Imperial Era and now considered one of China's national foods. Peking Duck is prized for the thin, crispy skin. It arrives to the table as a whole duck {complete with head and feet} and is sliced in front of us. A slice of the succulent duck skin along with a few sliced spring onions, a long wedge of cucumber and a dab of Hoisin sauce is placed atop a thin, hot pancake {served from bamboo steamer baskets}. Paul often jokes about how many ducks we "kill" {his word}, during each of our visits {I believe the record is six}, but after a 19-hour flight, it is when we arrive at our favorite restaurant- with our reserved duck waiting - that we know we have arrived in a very different world!

It is well mannered and expected to sample everything that is placed before us during a meal. {I mean... EVERYTHING!}

Dim Sum

Dim Sum is a Cantonese term for a meal involving small, individual portions of food, typically served in steamer baskets or on lovely little plates, only in the early morning and mid-afternoon hours. Because of the small servings, we can {and do!} enjoy sampling a wide variety of food. As with all Chinese meals, it is ordered family-style, served with a range of delicious dipping sauces. The dishes usually consist of a selection of dumplings, fried wontons, beef soup with minced garlic {yes, for breakfast!}, steamed buns, and creamy *Congee*. What Marcie craves most during our *Dim Sum* breakfast are the Chinese vegetables. Whether it is the crunchy Chinese Lettuce or another type of green vegetable, it always arrives steamed perfectly and served with a side of soy sauce. I have trouble, {as it is quite tricky} eating these with chopsticks but it is a dish that is well worth the effort.

Stories from Lands Afar

My very favorite person to travel with is my sister, Marcie. Not only is she my sister, but also my very best friend. I am lucky that she has been such a good sport traveling with me on each journey to China and Thailand. Her meticulous eye and creative insight is a great benefit to me and Coton Colors products as well. Because of this, she has plenty of stories to share.

In Marcie's words...

It truly is very difficult to begin to put into words the sights we have seen and the experiences we have shared while traveling overseas to China and Thailand. Each and every trip offers us a "new and different" perspective in one way and then a taste of what has now become "familiar and common" to us in another. These small snippets are my favorites of what I've seen, experienced and have come to love about the country of China.

Eating, watching movies, reading, needle-pointing and snoozing with 300 of our new closest acquaintances on the 19-hour flight over the top of the world {the longest leg of the 28-hour trip}... are an amazing way to begin our journey.

Border patrol, customs and entry into the country of China is very strict and militaristic. No smiling or joking going on in that job! Having our wonderful host waiting on us with luggage carts, bottled water and driver ready to whisk us off to our favorite restaurant for our first, five-hour Chinese dinner of the trip. We always {and I mean always} shut the restaurant down and often leave hours after the carpet has been steam-cleaned and every piece of furniture has been polished to a spit shine!

Breakfast - 7:30 am *Dim Sum* - arrives very quickly {especially if Paul has taken us to a typical 2:00 am spa treatment}. After eating we are off on our van ride to the factory, where the real fun begins. Chinese driving is NOTHING like driving in America. A three lane highway easily accommodates six cars as they merge and jockey around one another. This highway is often shared by cars, vans, container trucks, bicycles, motorcycles, plows, three-wheeled carts and people walking. Merge, stop, go, honk, jerk, bounce... all the norm, with countless close calls - and I mean close calls - in between. Driving "off" the "on" ramps of interstates isn't unusual, nor is watching a person cross eight lanes of traffic on foot, and people with teetering stacks of cardboard boxes or Styrofoam bungee corded to their bicycles. They make it work - no one is offended or upset - and we've not ever witnessed too harrowing of accidents!

Along the highway, once we leave the cities behind, the countryside is beautiful with small farms peppered throughout with perfectly manicured rows of vegetables and fruits growing. Chinese farmers still wear the straw hats and carry two watering cans on a stick on their shoulders. Picturesque to us, but also fundamental to the families and villages close by.

Factory visits are what these trips are about, meeting owners and seeing our product in production. We have been introduced over the years to the proper etiquette of conversing and engaging and usually enjoying food with many factory owners, who are our gracious hosts for tea and lunch. It is always so exciting to walk into a factory and see rows and rows of our product being produced. The very reason we are in China hits home and we are pleased!

Every time I return home from overseas, I realize that each and every trip is unique in some way. The layers of each of our trips has made my overall impression and encounter of China one-of-a-kind and unforgettable. I am truly blessed to have experienced firsthand the way of life and the means of industry in a country like China. In some ways we are all so very alike and...

Pig
Hard working home lovers.
Can sometimes be a little gullible.
1935 • 1947 • 1959 • 1971 • 1983 • 1995 • 2007

Rat
Charming, creative and sociable. Likes to gossip.
1936 • 1948 • 1960 • 1972 • 1984 • 1996 • 2008

Ox
Reliable and sensible, can be boring.
Good in business.
1937 • 1949 • 1961 • 1973 • 1985 • 1997 • 2009

Dog
Honest and loyal. Dislikes change.
Makes good friends.
1934 • 1946 • 1958 • 1970 • 1982 • 1994 • 2006

It's the Year of the...

Marcie and I have a great love of Asian art, getting lost {figuratively and a few times, literally} in the open air markets in China and Thailand. No matter if our travels are for business or pleasure, we always try to carve out some time to scour local art and have immensely enjoyed collecting it over the years. My favorite find, by far, is a set of 12 individual watercolors depicting the characters of the Chinese calendar. The combination of Chinese art and animals embodies my love of both. This grouping of individually framed pieces is always a point of conversation when guests are in my home.

Although I am in no way a believer in astrology, I am intrigued with how legends and mythology play a major role in Chinese culture and how the Zodiac {*Shengxiào*} influences the timing of life decisions for many of the country's people. The Chinese Horoscope is a 12-year cycle, with each year relating to a particular animal and its unique attributes. I keep a chart of the traits and characteristics of each animal and birth year in the top drawer of my dining room buffet. It's fun and makes for great conversation whenever I'm serving an Asian-inspired meal to pull the chart out and discover where guests fall... amazing how often the different characteristics align with our family and friends!

Tiger
Competitive and impetuous. Born leaders.
1938 • 1950 • 1962 • 1974 • 1986 • 1998 • 2010

Rabbit
Sociable, likes company. Good judge of character.
1939 • 1951 • 1963 • 1975 • 1987 • 1999 • 2011

Rooster
Proud and determined.
Can be seen as aggressive.
1933 • 1945 • 1957 • 1969 • 1981 • 1993 • 2005

Monkey
Versatile, inventive and mischievous.
Full of ideas.
1932 • 1944 • 1956 • 1968 • 1980 • 1992 • 2004

Dragon
Flamboyant, extravagant, imaginative, stylish.
1940 • 1952 • 1964 • 1976 • 1988 • 2000 • 2012

Sheep
Followers rather than leaders.
Diplomatic and affectionate.
1931 • 1943 • 1955 • 1967 • 1979 • 1991 • 2003

Horse
Sporty, sociable, uncomfortable around opposite sex.
1930 • 1942 • 1954 • 1966 • 1978 • 1990 • 2002

Snake
Charming and good mannered.
A bit lazy, perhaps venomous.
1941 • 1953 • 1965 • 1977 • 1989 • 2001 • 2013

menu

Steamed Pork Dumplings

Asian Sticky Ribs

Sesame Seed Salmon

Sweet Chili Noodle Salad

Stir Fry Zucchini
& Mushrooms

Grand Fortune Cookies

Steamed Pork Dumplings

Serves 8-12, Yields 42

Shaped like ancient silver and gold ingots and most traditionally prepared for families to feast upon at midnight on Chinese New Year, dumplings are symbolic of wealth and good fortune for the year ahead. —Susie

Dumplings:

1 pound	ground pork
1	(5 ounce) can water chestnuts, strained & finely chopped
¾ cup	scallions, finely chopped
4	garlic cloves, minced
1 tablespoon	sesame oil
1	egg, beaten
2 tablespoons	oyster sauce
1	(16 ounce) package wonton wrappers

Ginger Dipping Sauce:

½ cup	soy sauce
½ cup	balsamic vinegar
1 teaspoon	fresh ginger, peeled & grated
½ teaspoon	sugar

Dumplings:

Mix together all dumpling ingredients, except wonton wrappers. Fill the center of each wrapper with 1 heaping teaspoon of meat filling. Dip a small brush (or your finger) in a small bowl of water and wet edges of wonton wrapper. Fold over to create a triangle and pinch edges together so that the filling cannot escape. Place bamboo steamer in a large sauté pan. Fill the bottom with water, just below first layer of the steamer so the dumplings do not get wet.

Place dumplings 1-inch apart and steam until filling is cooked, about 20 minutes. Serve with Ginger Dipping Sauce.

Ginger Dipping Sauce:

In a small bowl, mix all dipping sauce ingredients well. Drizzle sauce over each dumpling.

Laura Says...
Simply
Steamed

I was inspired to bring my own bamboo steamers home from one of my early trips to China, after enjoying *Dim Sum* {and countless other Chinese dishes} from the baskets. Foods that are steamed require little or no added oils or fats, and they retain vitamins and minerals. They also absorb condensation, keeping water from dripping back onto the food. Bamboo steamers are widely available in popular grocery stores or kitchen supply stores and are quite inexpensive and easy to use. Don't be intimidated by working with a bamboo steamer; simply place the steamer into a pot of simmering water and steam until done. The bamboo baskets also make for on-theme serving pieces and can even provide an unexpected hostess gift. —Laura

Asian Sticky Ribs

Serves 8-12 appetizers

I made these for a party and everyone said they were the best baby-back ribs they ever had. That made me happy! It is just as easy to prepare several racks, so make plenty, and be sure to finish them on the grill. –Susie

2 ½ pounds	rack baby back ribs
12	garlic cloves, minced

Sauce:

¼ cup	molasses
6 tablespoons	honey
¼ cup	soy sauce
2 tablespoons	rice vinegar
2 teaspoons	sesame oil
1 teaspoon	five spice powder
¼ teaspoon	white pepper
½ teaspoon	black pepper
1 teaspoon	salt

In a medium saucepan, add molasses, honey, soy sauce, rice vinegar, sesame oil, five spice powder, peppers, and salt. Over medium heat, stir all ingredients until blended. Set pan aside to cool.

Remove the silver-colored membrane on the under side of the ribs. Start by sliding knife under membrane, then grab membrane with a paper towel, peel it back, and discard. Rub the racks of ribs with garlic and place in glass baking dish. Pour half of the sauce over the ribs, cover, and refrigerate for 8 hours. Pour remaining sauce in small bowl, cover, and refrigerate.

Remove ribs from the refrigerator and allow to rest for 20 minutes.

Preheat oven to 325 degrees.

Wrap the racks of ribs in aluminum foil and place on baking sheet. Bake for 2 hours. Remove ribs from oven.

Prepare and light grill. Remove cooked ribs from foil and discard drippings. Use the reserved sauce from refrigerator to baste and grill ribs for 4-5 minutes to finish.

Sesame Seed Salmon

Serves 8

This reliable recipe is weatherproof since it can be cooked on the grill or in the oven in the event of a downpour. By simply adding sesame seeds, it immediately enhances the flavor and appearance of the fish, giving the dish a much more extravagant presentation. Hooray for little effort! –Susie

2 pounds	salmon fillet, skin removed
	Kosher salt & pepper
½ cup	black and/or white sesame seeds
2 tablespoons	olive oil
	Sauce:
⅓ cup	soy sauce
⅓ cup	rice vinegar

Prepare and light grill. Create two aluminum foil pans using two 24-inch pieces of aluminum foil; fold each in half to make 12-inch squares. Bend edges up and pinch corners to form the pans. Repeat, and then place foil pans on baking sheet.

Cut salmon into 8 equal portions. Season fish with salt and pepper. Pour sesame seeds onto plate. Turn fish in seeds to coat evenly. Place salmon pieces on foil and drizzle lightly with olive oil.

In a small bowl, whisk soy sauce and vinegar together; set aside. Substitution for rice vinegar is to add 1 teaspoon of sugar to ⅓ cup of apple cider vinegar or white wine vinegar.

Slide grill pans off the baking sheet and onto the grill. Cook for 4 minutes per side or until slightly rare in the middle; flip using tongs and a spatula to keep salmon from falling apart. Keep in mind that when removed from the heat source, salmon will continue to cook.

Prior to serving, drizzle fish with soy sauce mixture. Serve with Sweet Chili Noodle Salad (see page 163).

Note: If broiling, adjust oven rack to the second from the top position and preheat the broiler to high. Follow instructions above, keeping the foil pans on the baking sheet while cooking.

Salmon Tips

- When selecting salmon, we suggest seeking fillets with a smooth appearance. Even if you have to drive a little out of the way for a fresh seafood market, you will find that they can direct you to the most palatable of fish.

- For this dish, select salmon pieces nearest to the head to get the most proportional fillets.

- Store fresh salmon in the coldest section of your refrigerator - the rear, typically. {You never use that stuff back there anyway!}

Be Inspired

While Laura has had the opportunity to bring pieces of Chinese pottery home from her travels, a local Asian market can provide a singular serving statement piece to tie your theme together. That's where we found this simple dragon plate. Good luck!

Sweet Chili Noodle Salad

Serves 8, Yields ½ cup

Have you ever eaten something and because it is so fresh and healthy you thought, "Wow... this is how I should eat all of the time!"? Well, that is how I feel about this Asian noodle salad. It is an unusual salad that has a bit of a kick and the peanuts are a must! –Susie

Noodle Salad:

3.75 ounces	rice noodles
1	carrot, peeled & thinly sliced lengthwise
1	seedless cucumber, thinly sliced lengthwise
1	small red onion, thinly sliced
1 cup	fresh cilantro leaves, chopped
1 cup	fresh mint leaves, cut in half lengthwise if they are large leaves
½ cup	dry roasted peanuts or cashews, coarsely chopped
2	limes, cut into wedges

Dressing:

2 tablespoons	soy sauce
4 tablespoons	sweet chili sauce
4 tablespoons	fresh lime juice
2 teaspoons	fresh ginger, peeled & minced

Cover rice noodles with boiling water in a medium bowl and let stand 8-10 minutes. Drain and rinse noodles under cool water. Place noodles in a serving bowl; top with carrots, cucumbers, onions, cilantro, and mint.

In a small bowl, mix all dressing ingredients together.

When ready to serve, drizzle salad with half the dressing and toss gently. Use the remaining dressing as needed. Sprinkle salad with peanuts and garnish with lime wedges.

Note: Not everyone likes spicy food, so I like to place a small dish of sweet chili sauce on the table in case someone wants more heat.

Stir Fry Zucchini & Mushrooms

Serves 8

Our sourcing agent, Paul - a fabulous cook and gracious host each time we are in China - sent us this recipe, and it is one of the adventuresome tastes of China we love. It is one of his favorites to prepare, and he frequently orders it for us during our travels. –Laura

1 ½ pounds	zucchini
7 ounces	mushrooms (assorted), sliced
1 tablespoon	oyster sauce
1 ½ tablespoons	water
¾ teaspoon	salt
1 ½ teaspoons	sugar
1 ½ tablespoons	vegetable oil
1	ginger root (approx. 3-inches), peeled and sliced into 4 pieces
2	garlic cloves, thinly sliced
1 teaspoon	cornstarch, dissolved in 2 teaspoons water

Cut zucchini in 2-inch long pieces. Next, cut each 2-inch piece in half lengthwise. Then cut halves into ⅜-inch slices.

In a medium pot, bring 8 ½ cups of water to a boil. Add mushrooms and return to a boil. Drain the water and set the mushrooms aside.

In a small bowl whisk oyster sauce, water, salt, and sugar; set aside.

Heat oil in a wok or large non-stick pan over medium heat. Add ginger and saute for 10 seconds. Add garlic and saute for 5 seconds. Add zucchini and saute for 2 minutes. Add mushrooms and saute for an additional 2 minutes. Then add the oyster sauce mixture and continue stirring until it comes to a boil. Add dissolved cornstarch. Stir until the sauce thickens slightly. Serve hot.

Fu
Blessing,
Good Fortune,
Good Luck!

Paul, ordering us a delicious meal in Hong Kong.

Before and after pictures Paul
sent us from his Shenzhen kitchen.

Grand Fortune Cookies

Serves 8

We made these giant cookies for Lynn's big 50th birthday and Laura and Milton wrote funny and appropriate fortunes for each person. Sometimes instead of inserting a message, I pipe chocolate pudding or whipped cream into the big cookies and garnish the plate with strawberries, pineapple and kiwi slices.

–Susie

1 ½ cups	all-purpose flour
1 ½ cups	sugar
3 teaspoons	water
3 teaspoons	vanilla extract
6	large egg whites

Spoon flour into dry measuring cup and level with a knife. Place carefully measured flour, sugar, water and vanilla (lemon or almond extract may be substituted for vanilla) in large mixing bowl and stir. In small bowl, whisk egg whites for 10 seconds before adding them to the flour mixture, and whisk until combined. Cover and refrigerate batter for 1 hour.

Preheat oven to 375 degrees and adjust oven rack to the middle position. Write your 8 messages on 8-inch slips of paper and set aside.

Locate a rolling pin or a large tube to use when shaping the cookies. Cover a large 17 ¼ x 11 ½-inch baking sheet with parchment paper. Using an 8-inch salad plate as a template, draw two separate circles on the backside of the parchment paper. Turn paper over and secure to baking sheet with masking tape.

Put ¼ to ⅓ cup of batter in the middle of each circle. Use a spatula to completely fill the circle with a thin layer of batter. Bake cookies for 5 minutes or until lightly golden brown around the edges. Watch closely to avoid overcooking. They are harder to shape and tend to break if they get too brown. Remove from oven and let them cool for only 10 seconds before using a metal spatula to gently but quickly loosen the edges of the cookies and remove from paper.

Place 1 cookie over the rolling pin or tube so that the edges almost touch. Be sure to put message inside cookie before shaping. Quickly slide cookie off rolling pin. Hold ends of the cookie in hands. Apply enough pressure to bend the cookie

A Well-Folded Accent

Though technically a Japanese tradition, the simple act of folding printed papers in your color scheme can add a beautifully artistic element to your Asian-themed event. *Origami* is a fun way to "garnish" plates and add an unexpected detail to your table settings. Simple instructions for a variety of shapes can be easily accessed online. Get folding!

in half. Remember, if the cookie doesn't bend easily, it may need to be placed in oven for 10-20 seconds to warm and soften before trying to shape. At any time if the cookie is too firm and not pliable, return it to the oven directly on the rack and allow it to warm before proceeding. Set the cookie over the rim of a large bowl to cool and keep shape.

Repeat the cooking and shaping process for the remaining cookies. Wrap each cookie in wax or parchment paper and place cookies in an air-tight container.

Note: I know this may sound involved, but once you get the hang of it, they are pretty easy and a lot of fun to make. Allow yourself some time to experiment or just make them with your guests or kids.

Cajun Sunday Supper

*Family traditions
served up
Louisiana style*

Family traditions served up...

I'm so lucky to have married Milton, 'the nice guy' {almost always}, and even more fortunate to have received in this union a wonderful mother-in-law, Marilyn. Of French descent, we lovingly call her *"Mère,"* meaning 'mother.' This name was passed from her mother who was raised on a plantation set along the Mississippi River just outside of New Orleans. Mère has the style, grace and charm one often associates with women living in the chic "Big Easy" in the 1930's.

Mère's roots certainly influenced the way my cooking style developed in the early years of my marriage. Her Cajun menus are still among our family's favorite Sunday night suppers. The one that my family most often requests for meals on Sundays is Rump Roast with Rice & Gravy served with Spinach Madeleine. Mère loves to tell the story of the first time I tried to create her Spinach Madeleine recipe. Milt and I were newly married and just beginning to cook together. Her spinach was one of my favorite dishes that she prepared so she happily gave me her recipe.

> " Live for today, laugh and dance, and tomorrow will take care of itself. "
>
> -Marilyn "Mère" Johnson

In making my list of groceries, I hesitated over an ingredient on the recipe card - 'Vegetable Liquor.' Not wanting to call her to ask {thinking I might look like an incapable new wife}, I set out for our local grocery store and scoured the aisles with no luck. I stopped by the adjoining liquor store and looked on every shelf, but still couldn't find it. The clerk was of no help when I asked him. Since this was before the convenience of cell phones, I drove all the way home, swallowed my pride and called Mère. She burst out laughing at my question... evidently vegetable liquor is the

seasoned water that remains in the pot once the spinach has boiled. Who knew?!?

Mère has always enjoyed being surrounded by those she loves the most - her three grown children, eight grandchildren and eight great-grandchildren... and counting. We all adore her and the times spent with her as well. For our children, we urge them to learn from and emulate Mère's kind, gentle nature. It has a lasting impact on those around her.

Our gatherings with Milton's family pay tribute to Mère's *N'Awlins* roots with great menus designed to serve a crowd; from the steaming mounds of crawfish to the big bubbling pots of gumbo. You'll always find lots of family, food and fun, with colorful stories swapped over traditional tastes most closely associated with the Crescent City... *Laissez les bons temps rouler!*

Flower of New Orleans

The *fleur-de-lis* is known for many reasons. It is the enduring symbol of Bourbon, France, the state of Louisiana, the city of New Orleans {and its beloved "Saints" football team to name but a few}. In French, *fleur* means flower and *lis* means lily and you can see the resemblance to a three petal flower. The three petals are said to represent faith, wisdom and chivalry. Today, the *fleur-de-lis* has taken on new meaning as a symbol of the rebirth of the city after Hurricane Katrina.

Mère's Cajun Culinary Memories

Over the years, I have enjoyed many of Mère's wonderful Cajun and Creole-style dishes which she has graciously passed on to me. She is a wonderful cook, a great teacher and she keeps a mighty clean kitchen. I will always cherish the colorful stories she has shared about her youth in the deep south of New Orleans.

In Mère's words:

Growing up in New Orleans - where good food is paramount to the second coming - leaves one with the desire to sample the gourmet and the simpler food alike. A favorite, which I could eat every day, was a boiled ham "Po-boy" sandwich made with freshly baked French bread {a must}, stacked ham, shredded lettuce and tomato. There is a legend that the secret ingredient which makes the bread so famous is the city's water supply. Who knows?

Sunday supper was always special. Everyone remained in their Sunday best as guests always came over after church. The table was set with the best china, silver and crystal. Most of the cooking had already been done and was usually rump roast, rice and gravy and vegetables. When the guests arrived, the children were allowed to greet them - a quick hello - then disappear until time for supper so the adults were free to enjoy their highballs and conversations. If an appetizer was served, I proudly passed the tray around, which made me feel very grown-up.

Monday in New Orleans was wash day. Everyone - including the restaurants - served red beans and rice for dinner. As long as the washing needed us home for the entire day, we might as well have been making dinner. Sausage, salad and French bread went well with this staple dish.

Every Friday night meant seafood. We began early in the day making seafood gumbo or getting shrimp, crabs or crawfish ready for the kettle. A special treat found us riding to the lakefront {Lake Pontchartrain} for huge piles of boiled crabs, crawfish or shrimp. This was served outdoors on long wooden tables and benches. Newspaper served as the table cloths - very, very informal and fun. After a dinner of buttery seafood juices dripping from your elbows, a bath after arriving home was certainly a necessity!

Many nights during the summer months, Daddy would pile us in the car and go for a "ride." This was mainly to cool off as it was so hot at home {without air conditioning}. He took this opportunity to ride around the city to view any new construction going on or anything of interest. Before heading home, the last stop was always Cloverland Dairy for ice-cream cones!

Another great summer treat was the Sno-ball truck. A truck would ride through neighborhoods ringing a bell. Children would come flying out with their nickels in hand. Deciding what flavor to choose was a major decision!

Our family left the French-influences of New Orleans for a short time to live in Lafayette, Louisiana - deep in Cajun country. This is where our family soaked up the wonderful culture and culinary arts of our Cajun friends. They taught us so many new ways to live and cook. Their food dishes were simple yet complex; knowledge of how to use spices and natural ingredients seemed to come from past generations. Above all, we learned... Live for today, laugh and dance, and tomorrow will take care of itself.

- Mère

Scalloped Oysters

This recipe comes to us from some of our favorite Coton Colors customers who also happen to be from the Cajun locale of Baton Rouge. Cajuns are known for being great cooks {and luckily are willing to share their recipes}! Sid Bowden Jr. and his wife, Bethany, are the owners of Holiday Hallmark and know a thing or two about Cajun cuisine. From their spirited LSU tailgates to their elaborate Mother's Day celebrations {it's been said that Bethany has never cooked the same recipe twice}, the Bowdens cook up Cajun at its finest.

Serves 10

1 quart raw oysters, undrained
6 tablespoons (¾ stick) butter
1 (8 ounce) package cream cheese, room
   temperature
½ cup Marsala wine
3 tablespoons green onions, chopped
½ teaspoon anchovy paste
½ teaspoon paprika
¼ teaspoon red pepper
¼ teaspoon salt
½ teaspoon Tabasco
2 tablespoons flat-leaf parsley, chopped

To prepare, pour oysters and juice in large skillet and simmer over medium heat for about 2 minutes or until edges just begin to curl. Drain and set aside. In a large skillet over low heat, add butter and cream cheese; stir until melted. Add wine and whisk until smooth. Stir in green onions, anchovy paste , paprika, red pepper, salt and Tabasco. Gently bring to a boil over medium-high heat, stirring constantly. Fold in oysters and garnish with chopped parsley. Keep warm and serve with crostini (see page 72).

menu

Swayze's Cajun
Crawfish Boil

Onion, Thyme & Goat
Cheese Tarts

Simple Arugula Salad
Seafood Gumbo

Bread Pudding with
Whiskey Sauce

Simply Served

When it comes to crawfish, no fancy serving platters are needed - newspaper is expected and will do just fine!

Crawfish Season

Crawfish season is from late-February to mid-May. Order from your local seafood market and use overnight delivery for live crawfish. Order crawfish to arrive the day before or the day of your crawfish boil. If you are feeding a smaller crowd, plan to order about 2 to 3 pounds of crawfish per person or 4 to 5 pounds for a heavier crawfish eater. And for those {like Mère}, who can't stop eating crawfish... you will need 5 to 7 pounds. Adjust seasonings for smaller batches.

Swayze's Cajun Crawfish Boil

Serves 8-12

Mère could practically eat her weight in crawfish... and she has passed this trait down to her grandchildren and great-grandchildren. Mary Parker and Sara Kate would eat crawfish all day long if they could, and even little Swayze, who is only two years old, happily enjoys them at family dinners! Milton makes the best crawfish for us and this is his recipe. –Laura

1	(35-40 pound) sack of live Louisiana crawfish
1	(26 ounce) box salt, for cleaning (purging)
5	(16 ounce) packages crawfish boil Seasoning {my favorite is Louisiana Fish Fry Products - Crawfish Crab & Shrimp Boil}
6-8	lemons, halved
6	medium onions, peeled & halved
6	garlic heads, halved

Empty crawfish into a cooler or large rubber tub with a removable drain plug. Clean (purge) crawfish by pouring the salt over top and covering crawfish with fresh water. Swish around for 3 minutes {not ANY longer or they will die!}. Drain water and spray crawfish with hose to rinse. Discard any crawfish that aren't alive.

Place a large stainless-steel boiling pot (30-quart) with basket insert over propane cooker. Fill ⅔ full with water.

Place basket in the pot. Add seasonings and vegetables. Bring water to a rolling boil over high-heat and continue boiling for 5 minutes to allow seasonings to mix thoroughly. Add crawfish and continue boiling for 5 minutes. Turn gas off and allow crawfish to soak in seasoned water for 30 minutes. Remove basket, pour out onto newspaper lined table and "have at it!"

Note: If your pot is not big enough then use two pots. Split ingredients in half and prepare pot as above. Cook first half of batch in one pot, remove and allow crawfish to soak while you cook second batch in another pot.

Onion, Thyme &
Goat Cheese Tarts

Serves 8

The sweet, caramelized onions and creamy goat cheese combine to make a savory, yet sophisticated tart.   –Susie

1	(16 ounce) box puff pastry dough, defrosted
3 tablespoons	butter
5 cups	onion (approx. 2 large onions), halved & thinly sliced
2	garlic cloves, minced
1 tablespoon	fresh thyme, chopped
	Sea salt & pepper
1	(4 ounce) log of goat cheese

In a large fry pan, melt butter over medium heat. Add onions, garlic, and thyme, and sauté for about 20 minutes or until golden. Season to taste with salt and pepper. Remove from pan and let cool.

Preheat oven to 425 degrees and adjust oven rack to middle position.

Unfold the dough on a lightly floured counter, and roll out to 8 x 16 inches. Trim the edges and cut into eight 4-inch squares.

Divide the onion mixture between the squares and spread on top leaving a thin border around the edges. Cut the cheese into 8 slices and place on top of the onions.

Place squares on a large baking sheet. Bake for 12-15 minutes until dough has risen and tart is golden brown. Remove from oven and let cool. Serve with a big glass of wine.

Note: No rolling pin? A bottle of wine will do the trick!

Chèvre: an artisan cheese

Chèvre, which means goat in French, is made from pure white goat's milk and is soft and creamy. It has a distinctively tart flavor when it is produced at the time the goats are feasting on summer clover and sunflowers. It is perfect for these tarts, potato salad or simply spread on a water cracker and topped with pepper jelly.

Simple Arugula Salad

Serves 8-10

This green salad is simply dressed with extra virgin olive oil and lemon juice.
The thin shaved pieces of Parmesan complete the salad perfectly. –Susie

1 pound	arugula, washed & dried
¼ cup	extra-virgin olive oil
2 tablespoons	fresh lemon juice
	Sea salt & freshly ground black pepper
1 pint	grape tomatoes (optional)
4 ounces	Parmigiano-Reggiano cheese, shaved

When ready to serve, place arugula in a large salad bowl. Drizzle arugula with olive oil and lemon juice. Sprinkle with salt and pepper; then toss. Top salad with tomatoes and shaved Parmigiano-Reggiano cheese. Toss and serve.

Mère & Milt dancing, 1984

We'll Have Big Fun on the Bayou

During her teenage years in New Orleans, Mère spent many evenings at the New Orleans' Cotillion Club dances held on the rooftop of The Jung Hotel, tagging along with her older sister, Olga, who claimed she often came uninvited! Of course, both of their dance cards filled up quickly every night {yes, they actually used those!}. As World War II was in full swing, Milton, an Ensign Flight Instructor, also perfected his renowned dancing skills by attending many USO hosted functions. As fate would have it, Mère met Milton on a "doomed" trip to Lake Pontchartrain. A group of teenagers headed out for an evening on the lakefront when their car got a flat tire. Mère smiles, recalling the long walk to the service station - the group taking turns rolling the inner tube with a stick. She and Milton connected and talked for hours. The two married within a year, her at the young age of 18. They spent 62 happy years as perfect dance partners.

Seafood Gumbo

Serves 8

My first dinner party where Seafood Gumbo was the main entrée ended up a disaster - I failed to take into account that all the guests were not from the South or had ever heard of gumbo. As I proudly ladled out their servings, one of my guests took one look and said, "I can't eat this dark stuff!" What to do? Holding back tears as I had only salad, French bread and dessert for the rest of the meal, I offered eggs. This did teach me to be alert as to whom I offered my cherished dish.   –Mère

No worries, this dish is over-the-top delicious. Mère's picky guest sure missed out on a fabulous seafood-rich Gumbo!

Roux:
1 cup	vegetable oil
1 cup	all-purpose flour
1	large onion, chopped
2	stalks celery, chopped
1	green bell pepper, chopped

Gumbo:
6 cups	hot water
1 pound	okra (fresh or frozen), sliced
1 teaspoon	salt
½ teaspoon	black pepper
½ teaspoon	cayenne pepper
1	bay leaf
1 pound	shrimp, peeled & deveined
1 pound	fresh crab meat, picked clean
1 pound	fresh crab claws (optional)
	Salt & black pepper, to taste
	Long grain white rice, cooked, for serving

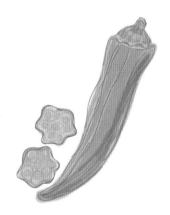

Roux:

Prep onion, celery, and bell pepper, and have readily available. Heat oil in heavy pot over medium-low heat. Slowly add flour a little bit at a time, stirring constantly. Constant stirring is a must! *Don't answer the door if there is a knock and don't answer the phone if there is a ring.* About half-way through the cooking process, the roux will become more liquid, but will thicken to paste consistency again as it nears completion. It may take about 45 minutes to 1 hour to reach this stage. It is very easy to burn a roux... if burning occurs, throw it out and begin again.

Throughout the years, I've enjoyed spending time with Mère and Big Milt in their home. When our first daughter, Kyle, was a newborn, we often found ourselves there... Kyle, prominently placed on the table in her infant seat. With all four of us seated around her, we watched her every movement as we enjoyed Mère's Gumbo. Kyle wasn't their first grandchild, but she was born at the perfect time - just as they both retired - and so she was fortunate to have their undivided attention. I remember Big Milt asking one time, "What in the heck did we look at before she was born?" What precious memories...

When the roux reaches the desired color, a rich brown {like a milk chocolate Hershey bar}, quickly add onion, celery, and bell pepper. Remove the pot from direct heat while continuing to stir. The heat of the roux will cook the vegetables. Keep stirring until vegetables are softened.

Gumbo:
Add hot water, okra, seasonings and bay leaf to roux. Stir well. Cover pot and lower heat, simmering at least 30 minutes. {You can let this sit for however long you'd like}. Just before serving, add shrimp, crab and crab claws and heat thoroughly, about 5 minutes. Do not over stir or overcook. You want to have nice lumps of crab. Shrimp will add liquid to pot; if gumbo is too thick, add hot water a little at a time. Season to taste with salt and black pepper, and add more cayenne pepper, if desired. Serve over long grain white rice with thickly sliced, crunchy French bread.

Note: The suggested ratio is ½ cup of cooked long grain white rice served with 1 cup Seafood Gumbo.

What is Chicory Coffee?

Chicory is the root of the endive plant, which is a type of lettuce, and this weedy plant with azure-blue flower can be found growing roadside. Just the root of the plant is roasted and ground. It is added to dark roasted coffee to soften its bitter edge. Coffee was first introduced to America by way of New Orleans back in the mid-1700's. The taste for coffee and chicory combined was developed by the French during their civil war. Coffee was scarce during those times, and they found that chicory added body and flavor to the brew. Cafe Au Lait is a delicious blend of Chicory Coffee with even parts milk poured out of two pots at the same time into one coffee mug. It is a real treat when served with delicious desserts such as this Bread Pudding.

Bread Pudding with Whiskey Sauce

Serves 12

The apples in this bread pudding "make it"... well that, and the awesome whiskey sauce. Use a good loaf of French or a five-grain Italian bread. The good news is, you can prepare the Bread Pudding and the sauce the day before and reheat it. It tastes fabulous the next day or even the next! It is even great out of the refrigerator cold, but the warm whiskey sauce is a must and with cold vanilla ice cream... it is pretty sweet!   –Susie

Bread Pudding:

1 loaf	robust bread, (approx. 16 ounces) cut into 1-inch cubes, crust on
4 cups	milk
4	eggs
2 tablespoons	vanilla extract
4 tablespoons	(½ stick) butter
2 cups	sugar
2	apples, unpeeled, cored & diced
1 cup	raisins

Whiskey Sauce:

16 tablespoons	(2 sticks) butter
2 cups	sugar
2	eggs, whisked
½ cup	whiskey

Bread Pudding:
Preheat oven to 350 degrees and adjust oven rack to middle position.

Place bread cubes in large bowl. Cover bread with milk. In a small bowl, whisk eggs and vanilla together, and pour over bread. Melt butter and pour ¼ cup butter in casserole dish and swirl to coat sides. Pour the remaining ¼ cup butter over the bread mixture. Sprinkle with sugar, apples, and raisins. Using a large spoon, gently fold ingredients until combined. Spoon bread pudding into a 2-quart glass casserole dish and place in oven. Bake for at least one hour or until the edges are bubbly and the pudding starts to pull away from the sides of baking dish. The top should be golden and slightly dome shaped.

Whiskey Sauce:
Place butter and sugar in a heavy medium sauce pan. Stir over medium heat until the butter is melted and the sugar is combined Reduce heat to medium-low. Quickly whisk the butter and sugar mixture while gradually adding the whisked eggs until blended. Remove from heat and stir ½ cup whiskey into sauce. Taste, and add more whiskey, if needed.

Sweet Grass Dairy...

Situated just a short distance from home, on 140 acres of rolling South Georgia pastureland, is Sweet Grass Dairy, a family-owned operation and one of the country's premier artisan cheese producers. Laura and Susie were fortunate to spend a morning on the Sweet Grass Dairy farm... an eye-opening adventure with a profound impact.

Al and Desiree Wehner opened Sweet Grass Dairy in 2000, starting with a small group of dairy goats and the milk from their grass-fed jersey cows. Their business began with a focused mission to show people a responsible way to dairy. Since the very beginning, Sweet Grass Dairy has been turning heads in the industry and has quickly gained acclaim for their cheeses and standards alike. Al and Desiree were joined in 2002 by their daughter and son-in-law, Jessica and Jeremy Little {and

their four young sons}, who own and operate the business today. With a goal to promote biological and sustainable agriculture, Sweet Grass Dairy runs on a rotational grazing system in which the cows graze lush pasture {a clear contrast to the concrete confinement barns most dairy animals call home}. Their philosophy allows cows to be cows, as they do not believe in overfeeding or over-stressing them for milk production. Sweet Grass Dairy simply makes the cheeses they are able to with the milk that their cows naturally produce. The system is far healthier for the animals, and for those fortunate enough to sample their cheeses... a farming business model which has proven to be popular and effective, but most importantly, respected.

Upon arrival, Laura and Susie encountered a herd of goats blocking the small gravel road leading

up to the farm. After a moment of laughter and patience, Laura gave her horn a slight honk... which apparently sounds just like the goats' dinner signal, as they immediately surrounded the car in curiosity, clearly looking for food. Not quite what they'd hoped to accomplish with the honk of the horn, but the laughter over the experience set the tone for the happy, relaxed day.

The private tour allowed Laura and Susie the opportunity to learn all about the Sweet Grass Dairy farming techniques. Most notably, they learned about the complex stages of artisan cheese making with the Sweet Grass Dairy team showcasing the process as a true art within itself. The many hands-on demands for each wheel of aged cheese and variables necessary to consider are overwhelming and inspiring. This industry - particularly when approached in the meticulous manner of Sweet Grass Dairy - is a true labor of love.

The uniquely flavorful Sweet Grass Dairy cheese selections are available to us in locally-owned markets and restaurants {and can most likely be found in your own hometown too}. If you are ever in the Thomasville, Georgia area, treat yourself to a taste of the many Sweet Grass Dairy products by visiting their Broad Street store - a cheese, wine and specialty food shop. And, if you're lucky enough to spend a morning in Thomasville, make arrangements to join one of the public tours of the Sweet Grass Dairy farm. It is educational and memorable for all ages!

After a morning on the farm, Susie and Laura headed to downtown Thomasville to visit the Sweet Grass Dairy storefront to discover endless tips on selecting and serving artisan cheeses.

- Sweet Grass Dairy produces a number of seasonal cheeses that will fit well into any menu and will certainly impress guests. The Asher Blue is a bold, cow's milk cheese, perfectly paired with a glass of port on a cold night, while the smooth texture of the Georgia Gouda - a young, raw cow's milk cheese - serves well for holiday festivities. The widely-popular Clayburne is closest in description to a mild cheddar; aged beautifully, Clayburne is only available during the holidays. The warmth of summer beckons different cheese flavors, such as Heat, an aged cows' milk cheese, smoked and blended with five different chilies. This cheese is perfect atop hamburgers or shredded for a Mexican meal. The Thomasville Tomme is a pleasant, rustic cheese, which is not overbearing during the heat of summer and is delicious served alongside sweet and savory appetizers.

- Almonds, olives, honey, Fig or Tomato Jam make perfect accompaniments for your cheese boards, as do in-season fruits, bringing out the flavors of the cheese and also making for a beautiful presentation.

- Take a different approach to displaying cheeses by cutting the selections into smaller servings - long, slender pieces, cubes and triangles - which creates a beautiful presentation and also limits the amount of fingers on the cheese.

- Don't wrap cheese in plastic wrap to store... instead use wax paper so the cheese can breathe and store it in the most moist area of your refrigerator - the produce drawer.

- Avoid serving processed cheeses, as they tend to be rubbery due to the high temperatures at which they are made. Instead, select raw milk cheese for better flavor and texture.

Easter Sweets & Treats

Cupcakes, cheer and the hunt for the Golden Egg

Cupcakes, cheer and the hunt...

By far, my favorite holiday is Easter, filled with memories of egg hunts and family traditions. I just love the green of the grass during the birth of spring in Florida and the anticipation of warm summer days ahead. I especially look forward to the celebration of hope and its special meaning to our family as we enjoy the church service together.

Since childhood, I have had a love-hate relationship with the Golden Egg. Don't get me wrong, I absolutely love the whole idea of this tradition. Every year the Easter Bunny hides our Golden Egg with its special "grand prize" treat tucked inside and this {not-so} little egg always gets the most attention. Much thought goes into each year's hiding spot and though our girls are well past the typical egg-hunting, basket-carrying age, they still eagerly anticipate the 'big hunt'... and somehow the prizes inside seem to get better each year.

> "Things are about to get serious..."
>
> -one sister says to another sister at the start of their hunt for the Golden Egg

In my early days, the Golden Egg was always part of the annual neighborhood egg hunt. My sister and I set out on the hunt for this special egg one Easter... knowing that the prize was the loveliest pair of sparkling rhinestone sandals we had ever seen. Once the hunt commenced I bypassed any inferior egg, keeping my full attention on the Golden Egg and soon finding myself with a bit of egg dilemma. Lucky me, I just had a feeling {call it a sixth sense for beautiful shoes}, that the egg was hidden in the top of the neighbors swing set. I can still remember the moment that I spied it with my little eyes and could envision nothing but those sparkly sandals on my feet. I reached up to grab the coveted prize and darn it, if my little arm was just too short to reach it. No matter how much I stretched up on my tippy toes, I just couldn't put my fingers on it.

What a predicament; I could not decide what to do… quietly leave my post, walk up to the nearest adult and calmly claim my right to the Golden Egg like the polite young girl my parents wanted me to be? Or should I stand by, defend my position and scream loudly that I was the rightful owner of the Golden Egg while kicking off my sister, who was suddenly clamoring up the swing set, just as anxious as I, to claim those shoes and the glory of finding the Golden Egg?

Needless to say, I chose the less polite path and I sadly stared out of the window of my bedroom {where I promptly found myself post-tantrum}. As a result, I developed a bit of jealously for the Golden Egg… and of my sister donning those shoes!

I know, I know… I need to put this injustice behind me and "step over it" as my mom loves to say, but I still get a bit of a competitive edge with my sweet sister when the Golden Egg is involved. Imagine my happiness at my unlimited supply of Coton Colors Golden Eggs {I've now designed ceramic, hand-painted Golden Eggs so all competitive children can develop a similar "love" of this family tradition}… and I've managed to buy myself a few pairs of lovely sandals through the years!

The Hendrix Family

The Golden Egg

Kristin, the dynamic Coton Colors National Sales Director, has two young, spunky daughters who have grown up with the Golden Egg. Each year it makes me happy to hear their stories of where, how and who found the egg. {Londyn, the youngest, finally won this year!} Ahhh… the sisterhood rivalry continues! —Laura

Keeping Egg Hunts Fair...
for Laura's Sake!

Hosting an annual egg hunt is always full of treats, but can also pose a bit of dilemma when kids' ages are mixed... especially when children are spirited {see aforementioned Golden Egg story!}. Older children tend to run and grab every egg in site, while shy, younger tots end up with empty baskets and sad faces. Egg hunts can be separated by ages, but it is a bit of a challenge to hide and execute. A family friend shared an idea that works well... use the color of eggs to dictate the hunt. Set a rule so that each child over age three can only find one {or two to three, depending on the size of your hunt} of each color egg. This will give your more competitive kids a goal while smaller, shy ones can have the time to gather their fair share. No tears necessary!

Deviled "Golden" Eggs

Serves 6, Yields 12

My mother-in-law is famous in her family for these deviled eggs. She recently taught my husband "how-to" and he has agreed to share the family secret with you. Sorry Bobbie, "the devil made him do it!" –Susie

8	eggs
¼ teaspoon	salt
⅛ teaspoon	fine black pepper
⅛ teaspoon	garlic powder (optional)
5 tablespoons	mayonnaise
3 tablespoons	sweet salad cubes
¼ teaspoon	sweet paprika, to garnish

Wash and place 8 eggs in pot and cover with cold water. Bring water and eggs to a boil and continue to boil uncovered for 15 minutes. Drain and return eggs to pan. Set pan in sink and run cold water over eggs. Peel eggs under cold running water and set aside.

Cut eggs in half lengthwise, and trim a thin slice off the bottom so the eggs sit flat on a plate. Using a small spoon, remove and place yolks in small bowl. Mash yolks with fork until they look like small fine grains without lumps. Stir in salt, pepper, and garlic to mashed egg yolks. Add mayonnaise and relish or salad cubes to the egg yolk mixture and combine until blended. The mixture should be smooth and creamy. Add more pickle juice if needed.

Use a small spoon to fill 12 of the 16 halves. Sprinkle with a pinch of sweet paprika.

Grapefruit Cupcakes with Whipped Berry Frosting

Yields 12 cupcakes

A sweet, Florida-inspired vegan cupcake created exclusively for The Happy Everything Cookbook by Jean Bates, owner of Lucy & Leo's, a famous Tallahassee cupcakery. —Susie

Whipped Berry Frosting

¼ cup blueberries
½ cup chopped strawberries
1 cup Vegan butter substitute
2-3 tablespoons soy milk
2 cups powdered sugar

Puree blueberries and strawberries in a food processor and strain juice; set aside. Using an electric mixer, beat butter substitute until creamy. Add 1 tablespoon soy milk. Gradually add powdered sugar and remaining soy milk alternately until smooth and creamy. Add berry puree to mixture until well combined. Spread or pipe onto cupcakes as desired. Top with fresh strawberries or blueberries.

1 cup	soy milk
1 teaspoon	apple cider vinegar
1 ½ cups	all-purpose flour
2 tablespoons	cornstarch
¾ teaspoon	baking powder
½ teaspoon	baking soda
½ teaspoon	salt
⅓ cup	canola oil
¾ cup	sugar
2 ½ teaspoons	vanilla bean paste
⅓ cup	grapefruit juice

Cupcake:
Preheat oven to 350 degrees and adjust oven rack to middle position. Line cupcake pan(s) with 12 paper liners.

In a medium bowl, whisk soy milk and vinegar together; set aside to curdle for 3 minutes. Using an electric mixer, beat together soy milk mixture, oil, sugar, and vanilla bean paste. In a separate bowl, sift together flour, cornstarch, baking powder, baking soda, and salt. Gradually add dry ingredients to the wet mixture and mix until well combined. Fold in grapefruit juice after ingredients have been thoroughly incorporated.

Fill cupcake liners ⅔ full, and bake for 20 minutes or until toothpick inserted in center of cupcakes comes out clean. Remove pan from oven and allow cupcakes to cool before frosting.

Note: Pure vanilla extract can be evenly substituted for vanilla bean paste.

Have Cupcakes, will travel ...

There's nothing like cupcakes on wheels to bring happiness to your Easter party! The trend of serving delicious, simple cupcakes {no forks or plates required!} is one that will surely stick around for many years to come. We're fortunate in Tallahassee to have access to a hometown cupcakery, Lucy & Leo's; and lucky for you, they agreed to share the delicious Grapefruit Cupcake recipe as one of their made-from-scratch flavors. Clearly passionate for all things sweet, owners Jean Bates and Paula Lucas cleverly create a variety of artfully-decorated, tasty cupcakes each day, and share them with our community from their popular bakery. On certain occasions {when we're really lucky}, Jean serves them from her festive cupcake camper, "Scotty" - a 1965 Serro Scotty Camper - which pulls up fully stocked with tasty treats to greet happy children {and adults} at local events and parties. Infusing Lucy & Leo's love of Florida citrus, this Grapefruit Cupcake with Whipped Berry Topping packs the perfect amount of sweet "Sunshine State" flavors to delight guests of all ages! The cupcake is truly delicious and I gotta say, Jean is one cool chick!

-Susie

Cinco de Mayo

Gathering girlfriends for a festive fiesta

Gathering girlfriends...

During my travels a few years back, I spotted a striking purple, hand-blown glass chandelier, and my creative soul had to have it for our home. I could almost instantly see the years of festivities we would share underneath the conversation piece. The chandelier was installed just in time to begin the tradition of an annual *Cinco de Mayo* celebration with my dearest girlfriends to commemorate our Mexican heritage... okay, we don't actually have any Mexican heritage, but the chance for great margaritas and tons of smiles shared with my closest *amigas* is plenty enough reason to celebrate.

I allowed that singular piece to set the stage for the celebration – which is key in any party. The colors of your home and your environment can do much of the decorating work for you. The beauty of a Mexican-themed fiesta – whether you celebrate it on the 5th of May or any day of the year – is that the ethnic flavors create the perfect amount of spice for a tangy event. For our menu, Susie simply called upon the indigenous tastes of a colorful country – foods that Mexico instantly evokes – margaritas, mangoes, limes, peppers and pork to provide the framework for a south-of-the-border celebration like no other.

> "When life gives you limes, make margaritas."
> -Jimmy Buffet

This out of the ordinary occasion was the perfect chance to cook alongside friends. Our own meal preparation involved all of our guests in the kitchen... from mixing their own Margaritas to blending the Mocha Chocolate Mousse and every dish in between.

And remember, while the Mexican menu will certainly be tasty, the refreshing laughter at this unexpected gathering with girlfriends is the most savory ingredient of all.

Hosting a Festive Fiesta

Beyond Fresh Flowers

Fresh flowers are beautiful for parties, but the cost can add up quickly, they can be challenging to work with and cut flowers are often a bit predictable. Incorporate these ideas to create beautiful, unexpected décor.

○ Succulents like Cactus or Bromeliads are fitting for a Mexican fiesta and they last, which means you can enjoy them for years after the party, or you can send them home with your guests as gifts from the occasion.

○ Handmade tissue flowers are also eye-catching, especially in colors that pop. Pouf these together along ceiling fans for a surprising look or use small versions atop colorful platters and vases.

As an added bonus, either of these options allow you {or as in our case, your teenage children} the opportunity to assemble several days prior to your event.

Party-Worthy Pottery

I'm fortunate to have an abundance of handmade pottery pieces I have made for the Coton Colors line through the years to pull together for our occasions. I love that the vibrant flavors of our parties often inspire future designs. In fact, I designed some of the Coton Colors pieces used in these pages after our very first *Cinco de Mayo* gathering. While my own collection is quite large {for obvious reasons}, just a singular handcrafted piece can be notable at your own event.

Will Work for Food

Don't feel as if all of the food has to be prepared before the party. A Mexican Fiesta is the perfect opportunity to try out Susie's unique form of entertaining. She "goes big" when planning the menu - including new recipes - and knowing she will have plenty of extra hands to help that night in the kitchen. The fun begins with the shopping. Carefully choosing the freshest ingredients and enjoying the journey… the stops at the produce stand, grocery, wine shop, bakery and even the seafood or meat market. Next, she returns home and washes the produce, piling it high in a bowl or basket making an easy centerpiece. When guests arrive there are plenty of fun aprons available and before you know it, people are begging to help chop and cook. It is a sight to behold. Guests love it; they laugh and drink wine; and it is always fun. This is a successful approach because everyone is somehow involved in the preparation and friends become more adventurous and much more confident about food and cooking because of it!

Invite Special Guests

Susie's sassy Chihuahua, Chica, happily answered my prissy Poodle, Posy's, invitation, even donning a sombrero for the fiesta. {The look on her face says that she LOVES the hat!}

In the company of friends...

The fun friends pictured among these pages are truly original Coton Colors customers. Along with countless others, these women, the ones I celebrate occasions with from the ordinary to the extraordinary, helped to set the stage for Coton Colors success. These friends indulged my passion for colorful, cheerful art. They showed up at all hours of the day in my garage/office to help in whatever way we needed to get my growing orders out of the door. They are the ones that hosted Coton Colors trunk shows – long before we were sold in storefronts throughout the US; their children were wearing the original Coton Colors hand-painted dresses; they and their requests led to many of the coveted pieces that still appear in our collection today. Endless thanks go to all the amazing women in my life… I'm always honored to host them in my home to show my appreciation for all they've done for me and this company.

– Laura

menu

Mix It Up Margarita Bar

Fried Green Plantains

Guacamole

Citrus Avocado Salad

Cumin Spiced Pulled Pork
with Mango Salsa

Mocha Mousse with
Lemon Cream

Mix It Up Margarita Bar
Strawberry Mint, Orange Jalepeño & Pineapple Ginger Margaritas
Serves 24

A Mexican menu instantly lends itself to a festive signature drink. Our Margarita Bar is likely among the most enjoyed aspects of our annual affair. Not only are the drinks unique and delicious, the presentation is appealing artistically, creating décor in itself. The act of each guest personalizing their own cocktail creates lots of energy and enthusiasm and the conversations mixed out of the creations are sure to make a memorable evening. –Susie

Flavored Syrups:

1 bunch	fresh mint
2	jalepeños
1	fresh ginger root (3-inch piece)
4 cups	sugar
4 cups	water
2 cups	fresh strawberries, sliced
2 cups	fresh squeezed orange juice (approx. 6 oranges)
2 cups	fresh pineapple, cubed

Margarita Base:

12 cups	tequila, divided
8 cups	triple sec, divided
4 cups	fresh lime juice (approx. 32 limes), divided

Set three medium bowls on counter. Chop fresh mint and place in first bowl; set aside. Using a fork, stab the jalapeño four times; leave the fork inserted in the jalapeño to weigh it down when placed in the bottom of the second bowl. Repeat for the second jalapeño and place in same the bowl. Finally, peel and cut ginger into thin disks and place them in the third bowl.

Aguas Frescas

Another great thing about this "bar" is that kids or guests not partaking in the margaritas can make yummy fruit sodas by mixing the fruit syrups with club soda or lemon-lime soda. These are very similar to the authentic *Aguas Frescas* served and enjoyed throughout Mexico. Fun for all ages... a little "happy" for everyone!

In a large pot, combine 4 cups of sugar and 4 cups of water. Cook over medium-low heat, stirring continuously until mixture is hot and sugar has dissolved. Pour equal amounts (approx. 1 ½ cups) of syrup in each of the three bowls. Allow syrup to infuse 45 minutes or until syrup is cool enough to refrigerate. Strain each syrup and pour each into separate resealable containers, label with name and refrigerate until ready to use.

In a blender, puree 2 cups of strawberries with the mint syrup. Pour the strawberry mixture into a small pitcher, cover, and refrigerate. Next, mix orange juice with jalapeño syrup in a small pitcher, cover, and refrigerate. Finally, puree 2 cups of fresh pineapple with the ginger syrup. Pour the pineapple mixture into a pitcher, cover, and refrigerate.

Before serving, in a large (12 cup) beverage container or two pitchers, mix half of the listed ingredients to make the margarita base. {No need to make all 24 cups of margarita base at one time.} Mix in 6 cups of tequila, 4 cups of triple sec and 2 cups of fresh lime juice to yield 12 cups.

Prepare the bar with items needed such as glasses, dishes with salt, garnishes, ice bucket, ice, club soda. Place the three pitchers of fruit syrups and the container of margarita base on the bar.

Encourage guest to help themselves. Use a lime to rub the rim of each glass. Dip the rim into salt while turning glass slowly. Fill glass with ½ cup of ice. The typical mix ratio is at least two parts margarita base to one part fruit syrup. Stir, taste, and adjust with more base or syrup. Try topping with a splash of club soda.

Set the Bar

Other helpful hints...

- Use an electric juicer to squeeze all of the limes for the margarita base in advance.

- Freeze any left over lime juice for future use.

- Chill the bottles of tequila and triple sec so that the margarita base doesn't melt the ice.

- Collect different bottles and make clever labels for the syrups. Incorporate your favorite herbs or fruits to create your own margarita flavors.

- Maybe try cilantro and cucumber, lavender and peach... experiment, but most importantly, have fun!

- Pre-make garnishes for margaritas with pieces of fruit and herbs that were used to make each flavor.

- Hand write cards that describe each garnish.

Fried Green Plantains

Serves 8, Yields 24 pieces

I have enjoyed eating fried green plantains {Cuban 'Tostones'} ever since I was a little girl during our many visits to Key West. Plantains are popular in Mexico too! Some people {like my husband, Ed} prefer the sautéed, sweet, ripe plantains, but my favorite are the green plantains served fried, sprinkled with sea salt and a squeeze of lime... 'muy fabuloso'!   –Susie

3	green plantains
4 cups	vegetable oil
2 tablespoons	salt
	Sea salt, to garnish
3	limes, cut into 24 pieces, to garnish

Use a sharp knife to cut the ends off of the plantains. Peel plantains, by scoring the skin lengthwise in four places. Then, using a knife and fingers, pull peel away. Cut plantains into 1-inch pieces.

Heat oil in 10-inch cast iron skillet over medium-high heat. Fry 8 plantain slices for 4 minutes and drain on a paper bag. Fry the remaining plantain slices in batches of 8. Allow plantains to cool slightly and smash each piece of fried plantain with a mallet or the palm of hand to a quarter-inch thickness.

Fill a large bowl with 8 cups of water and season water with 2 tablespoons of salt. Soak fried smashed plantains for one minute in salty water, remove them from water, and then drain on paper towels.

Re-heat oil in skillet and fry each batch of plantains again for 4 or 5 minutes until crisp. Drain on paper bag and sprinkle with sea salt. Plantains taste best with a squeeze of lime.

Hint: To tell if your oil is hot enough to fry, put a few popcorn kernels in the oil and when they pop the oil is ready.

Better with Age

Plantains are most typically served cooked, unlike soft sweet bananas that we are accustomed to enjoying raw. A staple food source in most tropical areas of the world, plantains are larger, firmer and lower in sugar than bananas. The unripened "green" plantain is prepared much like a potato and is usually fried, but can also be steamed or boiled. Ripe plantains {yellow-black in color} are soft in texture and have a much sweeter taste, making them frequent ingredients in dessert dishes. In contrast to most fruits and vegetables that spoil quickly, plantains are a great value because if you purchase them green, you can slice and make chips or *Tostones* immediately or if a week passes and you haven't had the chance to prepare them... chances are they will have ripened perfectly for you to slice and sauté them for something sweet.

Guacamole
Yields 2 cups

This guacamole should be chunky and not entirely smooth or mashed. Make sure that you use ripe black Hass avocados. There seems to be some debate about whether adding the avocado pit to the guacamole will prevent it from turning brown... but, why take the chance? Put a pit or two in the bowl and enjoy guacamole with tortilla chips. –Susie

⅓ cup	sweet onion (1 small), minced
2	jalapeños, seeded & minced, divided
⅓ cup	cilantro leaves, chopped
1 ¾ cups	Hass avocados (approx. 5 small)
2 tablespoons	lime juice (approx. 2 limes)
1 teaspoon	Creole seasoning
½ cup	tomato (1 medium), diced

In a medium bowl, place onion, 2 tablespoons minced jalapeño, and cilantro.

Cut avocado lengthwise all the way around to the pit. Twist avocado in opposite directions to separate the two halves, remove pit, and set aside. Score the avocado flesh and then squeeze ripe avocado into a bowl. Repeat until avocado flesh measures almost 2 cups.

Gently fold avocado into onion mixture. Next, stir the lime juice and Creole seasoning into the avocado and fold in the tomatoes. Taste and adjust seasoning with more jalapeño, lime juice or Creole seasoning, if needed. {My Texas friend says no salt and pepper!}

If covered, it will keep in refrigerator 1 hour.

It's Not Easy Being Green

The flavor and texture of your Guacamole will be completely determined by the avocado you choose {no pressure!}. Avocado selection and handling can be a bit challenging. It is very important to use purplish black Hass avocados that have pebbly skin and should give to the touch, but not be too soft. Once you have them home, don't ever refrigerate avocados, as this keeps them from ripening properly. Instead, place unripe avocados in a brown bag near natural light and within 5 days they should be perfect for preparation. If the inside is soft and a pale gold color, the results will be a creamier guacamole.

Citrus Avocado Salad

Serves 8-12

Our friend and favorite local caterer, Paula Kendrick, kindly contributed a few zesty recipes to this party. Well-aligned with my philosophy of bringing girlfriends into the kitchen, Paula generously swapped culinary techniques and cooking tips with our group to prepare her Citrus Avocado Salad recipe, an easy and healthy dish with Florida-fresh flavors. –Susie

3	ripe avocados
1	ruby red grapefruit
2	naval oranges
1	jalapeño, seeded & diced, divided
½ cup	cilantro, chopped (optional)
½ teaspoon	sugar
½ teaspoon	kosher salt

Cut avocado lengthwise all the way around to the pit. Twist avocado in opposite directions to separate the two halves, remove pit and set aside. Score the avocado flesh and cut into cubes.

Peel and section the grapefruit and oranges; cut them into pieces.

In medium bowl, combine avocados, grapefruit, oranges, half of the jalapeño, cilantro, sugar, and salt. Taste and add more jalapeño, if desired.

Spoiled by Florida Citrus

Laura's childhood home in Miami had an old grapefruit tree, which was covered in fruit during winter months and not far away, her grandmother had a number of huge orange trees in her own yard. Fresh fruit was as simply accessible as a quick stroll in the yard to pick a fresh grapefruit right off the tree, and hand-squeezed orange juice flowed throughout the "winter time" of South Florida.

Cumin Spiced Pulled Pork with Mango Salsa

Serves 8

There are plenty of ways to serve this pulled pork. It is great on top of Corn Fritters {see page 239} or with warmed tortillas. I also suggest trying it on a bun with Pickled Onions and Mango Salsa, served with Simple Slaw. But, my favorite idea is to serve leftover pork the next morning {so make more than you need} over cheese grits or hash-brown potatoes with a fried or soft poached egg on top, and don't forget the warmed tortillas! Thanks, Paula, for this delicious and versatile recipe. –Susie

4-5 pound	pork butt
2 teaspoons	ground cumin
	Ground black pepper
2 cups	pineapple juice
¾ cup	soy sauce
¼ cup	balsamic vinegar
2 tablespoons	olive oil
2 tablespoons	honey
4 teaspoons	fresh ginger, peeled & minced
1	Vidalia onion, finely chopped
1 bunch	fresh cilantro, chopped
3	fresh jalapeño peppers, seeded & chopped
6	garlic cloves, minced
	Salt & coarsely ground black pepper, to taste

Rub pork butt with cumin and pepper and place in an extra-large glass or plastic bowl. In another large bowl, combine pineapple juice, soy sauce, balsamic vinegar, olive oil, honey, ginger, onion, cilantro, jalepeños, and garlic. Pour mixture over pork, cover and refrigerate overnight for 12 hours, turning pork once.

Preheat oven to 325 degrees.

Pour half of marinade from pork into small bowl, cover, and refrigerate.

Bake pork in large roasting pan, covered for 3 ½ hours. Remove from oven. Uncover, allow pork to cool slightly, and use a fork to shred meat. Discard pan drippings. Place shredded pork in clean pan.

Boil reserved marinade for 5 minutes. Pour desired amount of boiled marinade over pork.

Susie's Mom Shares... Simple Slaw

Cut one head of cabbage into thin shreds and mince one small onion. Place cabbage and onion in large bowl. In a small jar with lid, place 3 tablespoons of sugar, 1 teaspoon of salt, ¼ cup vinegar, and ½ cup of mayonnaise. Seal jar and shake until well mixed. Pour dressing over cabbage and onion and season with salt and plenty of fine black pepper. Cover and refrigerate until chilled or serve the next day.

Return pork to oven and roast uncovered until crisp. Add additional cumin, salt and pepper to taste. Serve with Mango Salsa (see page 220).

Hint: Top it off with Pink Pickled Onions for added flavor and color. To prepare, thinly slice a red onion and place into a resealable bag. Squeeze the juice of one lime over the onion, add a pinch of salt and toss. Refrigerate for at least six hours, or until the onions are soft and bright pink. These will keep approximately three days chilled in the refrigerator and also make a great addition to a cheese board.

Friends with Good Taste

Paula generously invited us into her catering kitchen at the Black Fig to savor the flavors of this recipe. Alongside co-owner, Mark Suber, they opened the Black Fig and have quickly created a locally-favored culinary destination with a gourmet-to-go business in addition to their thriving catering business. When time for party preparation runs short, we often count on the Black Fig to serve up fabulous tastes.

Mango Salsa

Serves 8-10, Yields 4 cups

Like Jimmy Buffet sings in "Son of a Sailor", we shook the hand of the Mango Man on a family trip to Cabo San Lucas a few years back. The simple act of skinning and scoring the succulent fruit, dousing it with a bit of lime and adding a touch of sea salt... yum! Makes my mouth water even now. Our kiddos walked around gnawing mangoes off of a stick for much of the trip, and now, anytime we serve this Mango Salsa, the memory sharing abounds. –Susie

2	large fresh mangoes, peeled & diced
1	small sweet Vidalia onion, finely chopped
¾ cup	fresh cilantro, chopped
1 teaspoon	lime zest
¾ cup	lime juice (approx. 6 limes)
1 teaspoon	ground coriander
2	garlic cloves, minced
	Salt & coarsely ground black pepper, to taste

In a medium bowl, combine all ingredients. Season to taste with salt and pepper. Stir thoroughly.

Note: This Mango Salsa - also Paula's recipe - has a kick! Serve with pulled pork, fish tacos, or as a "go to" salsa with tortilla chips.

Look... the Mango Man!

Cutting a Mango

The following steps make cutting this juicy fruit quick and simple...

- Cut the mango along either side of the pit {which is oblong in the center of the fruit}, leaving three pieces... two 'halves' and a middle with the pit.
- Place the halves, skin down on the cutting board and cut a crosshatch pattern, without cutting through the skin.
- Holding onto one half of the mango with two hands, push the fruit upward while pulling down on the skin. From here, slide the knife between the skin and flesh to completely cut the mango pieces from the skin.
- Lay the pitted piece flat on the cutting board and use a paring knife to remove the pulp from the pit.

Mocha Mousse with Lemon Cream

Serves 10-12

Coffee, chocolate and lemon are some of my favorite ingredients and this is one of my most loved desserts because it is surprisingly light and the perfect rich chocolate fix after a big meal. The mousse needs to be made at least two hours ahead, but because it is made in a blender, this dessert couldn't be easier or more fun to make.   –Susie

Mocha Mousse:

2 cups	(16 ounces) bittersweet or semisweet chocolate chips
1 ½ cups	(12 ounces) strong decaffeinated coffee, hot
¼ cup	sugar
6	egg whites

Lemon Cream:

1 cup	(8 ounces) whipping cream, chilled
1 ½ teaspoons	lemon zest, divided
2 teaspoons	fresh lemon juice
2 tablespoons	sugar

A Peppermint Twist

To tie in flavors of the holiday season, crush peppermint candies and use these in place of the lemon zest and lemon juice to make a Peppermint Cream.

Mocha Mousse:

Brew coffee. In a blender, combine chocolate, hot coffee, and sugar. Cover with lid and process for 10 seconds. Add egg whites, cover tightly, and blend on high for at least one minute. Pour chocolate mixture into 8 small bowls and refrigerate for 2 hours, until set.

Lemon Cream:

In medium bowl, place cream, lemon zest, juice, and sugar. Whisk cream by hand until soft peaks start to form. If it gets too stiff, add a bit more cream.

Serve chocolate mousse with a dollop of Lemon Cream. Garnish with lemon zest.

Hint: I always use bittersweet chocolate, because I much prefer dark chocolate. If you like milk chocolate, use semi-sweet chips and, of course, you can always use regular coffee.

Alligator Point Beach Weekend

Sun-soaked, spontaneous dining on Florida's undiscovered coast

Sun-soaked, spontaneous dining...

There is something about the sound of waves and water that just evokes happy memories for me. Growing up in the Miami sunshine, we spent most of our time in a pool or on a boat. Parties around the pool were spontaneous, picnics on the beach were a regular occurrence, and jaunts down to fish or lobster in the Keys were common. As I headed "north" {in Florida, that is} for college, I can recall a slight anxiety about leaving the sea behind. Luckily for my sun-soaked soul, it didn't take long for me to find North Florida's undiscovered coast just south of Tallahassee.

Nearly a decade ago, my extended family was lucky enough to land on Alligator Point, purchasing a house that quickly became a gathering place... the spot where we leave the hustle and bustle of life behind and take time to relax and reconnect. The idea of a nearby place for us all to be together for impromptu weekend getaways and holidays alike was truly the root of our desire in creating a family beach home.

I have fallen in love with the natural beauty of Alligator Point's relaxed, sandy shores. The towering pine trees and dense palmettos of the Apalachicola National Forest back right up to the Gulf waves where the wildlife is abundant, providing endless up-close encounters as nature just happens by. The locale provides a number of vantage points... our dock on the Point is the perfect vista to watch as osprey, bald eagles and dolphins fish for their own dinners. From the boat, we spy numerous sea turtles, giant rays and tarpons swimming by. And from our screened porch, we are always surprised to see the resident garbage-hungry black bear sauntering down the crushed shell road as he pays us an unwelcome visit.

> " If you're lucky enough to be at the beach, you're lucky enough! "

This is not a coastline that would suit everyone. Depending on your point of view, there is nothing much to do and nowhere to shop. But when I am here, I know that I wouldn't want to change places with anyone in the world.

All six of the cousins {and the six "grand-dogs"} have spent their adolescence at this beach, willingly spending time with family, simply being together. The girls have learned to drive in the rag-top Jeep that Milton insisted we had to have as a 'beach mobile'; multiple bright red strawberries appeared on their legs and arms after hours of tubing behind the boat; and eventually, they've spread their own water wings and taken our family boat, the 'atta girl, to the Gulf... for their own successful fishing adventures.

This is the place where we can truly "be as we are". During the short hour drive from the "city", makeup and hair dryers are quickly replaced with sunscreen and pony-tails. As we cross over the Ochlockonee Bay Bridge we find ourselves catching our breath as we anticipate the memories that await us. Cell phone service is {gratefully} spotty and beach neighbors just tend to surface. It is along these beaches and on the tip of the sandy Point that gatherings simply just happen. Vehicles are replaced by boats, with the wide expanse of saltwater serving as a much quicker 'road' to bring friends together. Tables are large enough to accommodate an unexpected crowd, and they frequently aren't set until moments before the meal is served... stragglers tend to arrive as the smell of the grill permeates the air.

Continued...

'Atta Girl!

Although we don't have a large yacht, rather the opposite - a small boat we use to ski and fish from - it still felt deserving of a name. The fitting title came rather easily. Whenever his girls tell my Dad {G-Daddy to his granddaughters} news of good things we have done - recent accomplishments, overcoming of struggles or really, any good news - the first thing that he proclaims is always, always...

'atta girl!

This affirmation just does something for my soul, and I never tire of hearing it.
–Laura

Life moves at a maddening pace at times, yet for a brief moment we are able to leave it behind... adults barter cooking and clean-up duties with the girls in competitive games of Continental Gin; we laugh hysterically as we attempt to teach friends to ski in the bay; the wee hours of the night echo with laughter from the girls' bunk room {and the personalities of the girls come out... six teenagers in one room equals lots of character}. Mornings find me preparing breakfast alongside my parents and enjoying coffee on the porch together in our pajamas... a luxury not possible in daily life though we live just a few miles apart at home. At the beach, time just stands still... enough to reconnect before chaos continues.

It is in this place of sunshine and smiles that I most enjoy cooking; the pace is relaxed and with my sister in the kitchen beside me, we indulge in the luxury of trying new recipes in addition to preparing coastal favorites. It does take some foresight and a well-stocked pantry of basics as there are no grocery stores within

miles, but each evening brings us the flexibility to cook the catch of the day. Menus are created based on fishing luck and the guest count is dependent upon the friends you pass by on the boat. The people, the place, the lifestyle... they always seem to align for a fun gathering perfectly poised for happy memories.

Our beach home is the one to which our girls will one day bring their own children, in hopes that the cycle of Florida life will continue, as a new generation embarks on their own

sun-soaked memories. The recipes shared in this chapter can be enjoyed wherever you find your own slice of paradise. These simple to prepare dishes are sure to please each sunburned guest at your own impromptu gatherings.

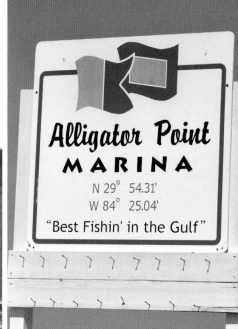

The Journey is the Reward

While one of the best things about our beaches is the lack of commercialism – no high-rise condos or crowds of tourists – the quaint, small-beach life can have one drawback... no nearby grocery stores. Years of beach trips have taught us to not only plan ahead before leaving the city, but also to carve out time to make key stops along the way. We always have a number of 'coastal characters' we visit during the short drive. The people we meet have the best stories {and advice} and are always happy to have our business.

LAURA'S STOPS:

- *"City" Grocery Store* - visiting the last major supermarket before the traffic lights disappear to a two-lane highway. This is the last resort stop for ingredients not likely to be found along our beach. If a recipe calls for cilantro or feta, better buy it before leaving town... and don't forget the mandatory Tootsie Pops for on-board boat treats.

- *Mineral Springs Seafood Market* - this friendly seafood shop provides their famous stuffed shrimp and delicious dips made from local fish smoked in their parking lot in addition to fresh off the boat seafood {though we hope our own fishing luck will prove plentiful for our meals}.

- *Angelo & Son's Seafood Restaurant* - to pick up a bottle of their to-die-for Greek Salad Dressing {and a walk down memory lane as this is where I had my first date with Milton}.

- *Local produce stand* - my favorite place to pick up locally-grown seasonal fruits and vegetables is from any dirt-floored, wholesome roadside stand. We always grab juicy watermelons to serve while swimming on our sandy offshore reef, vine-ripe Florida tomatoes and fresh, sweet white corn for grilling. {White is the only corn that mom lets me buy}.

MILTON'S STOPS:

- *Mike's Marine Supply* - for those boat "must-haves" that he can't live without... because every responsible boater should be prepared, right???

- *Crum's Mini Mall* - tinkering through this store to "replenish" his overflowing tackle box and purchase anything else under the sun {literally, ANYTHING!}.

- *"The BP"* - the last gas station, located at the bridge, for live bait {shrimp and pin fish are a must for the type of fish we plan to catch}, bags of ice and cold beer of course... plus for a bit of socializing with friends we happen upon coming from or going to the beach.

- *The Boiled Peanut Man* - to pick up the irresistible boiled green peanuts sold roadside {hopefully at the Alligator Point cutoff road} and scooped to order out of a boiling hot pot. A perfect traditional southern snack to share with guests - if we don't eat them all first!

Tallahassee

Dee fishing for her dinner, 1966

The girls with G-Daddy & DeeDee, 1991

Marcie, Laura & Jay on Key Biscayne, 1968

Time flies when you're having fun at the beach!

Sara Kate, Mary Parker & Caroline are ready for the July 4th boat parade, 2001

Bathing beauties, Kyle & Logan... slathered in sunscreen, 1993

Mary Parker seeking sea creatures ...with her pal Briggs, 2003

Sara Kate and Laura enjoying the always-present Tootsie Pop, 1993

Lots of fishies in just one small scoop... Mary Parker & Sara Kate, 2004

Alligator at the Point...

Boat rides to the sandy reef {five miles offshore} take us past this view of the treeline on the west end of the Point. Perhaps the alligator shape the pine trees form is the clever reason why this area is named Alligator Point? Meeting time at the reef is always at the low tide of the day when the depths at two to three feet are perfect for floating and swapping stories, with hundreds of sand dollars at our feet. High tide finds us on the tip of the Point on a sandy spit where we enjoy secluded picnics complete with hibachi grill, hotdogs and grilled pineapple... a delicious, shoreside feast.

menu

Watermelon Margaritas

Smoked Fish Dip

Crab Fritters

Potato Salad with
Goat Cheese & Capers

Head-on Shrimp

Peach Cobbler

Watermelon Margaritas

Serves 6

This recipe is dedicated to our friend Jennifer Yaun Langford who was the Jefferson County Watermelon Queen back in the late 70s! It's a perfect Fourth of July fun drink! –Susie

4 cups	seedless watermelon chunks
¾ cup	tequila
1 tablespoon	triple sec
3 tablespoons	fresh lime juice (approx. 2 limes)
4 tablespoons	sugar, divided
6 cups	ice, crushed
1	lime, cut into 12 pieces, for garnish

Place watermelon, tequila, triple sec, lime juice, and 2 tablespoons of sugar in blender and purée until smooth.

Put 2 tablespoons of sugar in a small dish. Use a lime wedge to rub the rim of each 12 ounce cocktail glass. Dip the rim into sugar while turning glass slowly.

Fill glasses with crushed ice. Pour Watermelon Margarita into each glass, and garnish with a lime wedge.

Cooling Off

Located a few miles from our hometown, Jefferson County is acclaimed as a top producer of watermelons, offering a sweet abundance of some of the juiciest watermelons in the South. The rich soil and warm weather prove perfect for growing watermelons, and so we're rather spoiled by the accessibility of the fresh fruit... perfectly messy for a hot day on the beach. No matter where your source, be sure you pick up a watermelon as you head off on your own summer beach soirées. Store deep in your cooler and pull out the ice cold treat to please your entire crowd... from babies to grandparents, the succulent fruit cools everyone off and a whole watermelon makes a happy last-minute gift for your beach hostess.

Smoked Fish Dip

Serves 8-10, Yields 2 cups

Delicious smoked fish is easily accessible at local seafood markets, but many of the menfolk in our lives take great pride in the process of smoking fish. They are happy to spend much of the day building their smokers and enjoy plenty of beer and the company of one another as the fish cook. We don't mind too much... smoking the fish for this dip is a great use for the multitude of fish that fill our freezers! –Susie

1 cup	smoked fish
¾ cup	mayonnaise
2 tablespoons	sweet pickle relish
2 tablespoons	celery, minced
½ cup	sweet onion, grated
1 tablespoon	fresh lemon juice
⅛ teaspoon	garlic powder
	Salt & pepper, to taste
	Saltine crackers

In a medium bowl, mix all ingredients together. Season to taste with salt and pepper. Serve with saltine crackers.

Note: Shop your local seafood market for smoked fish. Try mullet, amberjack, even salmon... any smoked fish will work. Call ahead to check for best selection and availability.

Bikini baby, Laura, with her barracuda catch of the day, 1966

Crab Fritters

Serves 6, Yields 12 fritters

Adapt this fabulous recipe for non crab-eating guests by substituting two ears of fresh corn for the crab. Cut the corn off of the cob and gently saute in the fry pan with 1 tablespoon of olive oil for 3 minutes. Place corn on plate to cool and wipe pan clean. Continue with the crab fritter recipe steps. –Susie

1 cup	all-purpose flour
¼ cup	cornmeal
1 ½ teaspoons	baking powder
½ teaspoon	salt
2 teaspoons	Old Bay seasoning
½ cup	buttermilk
2	eggs, whisked
3	green onions, white & light green parts chopped (optional)
1	(16 ounce) container lump crabmeat, shell removed
4 tablespoons	vegetable oil, divided
	Sea salt, to taste
	Hot sauce, to serve

Mix flour, cornmeal, baking powder, salt, and seasoning in a medium bowl. Gradually stir buttermilk and eggs into flour mixture. Next, add onions and crab to batter, gently folding until combined.

Heat 2 tablespoons of oil in a large nonstick pan over medium-high heat. Make 6 mounds of batter in the hot fry pan; each mound should be 3 tablespoons of batter. Press fritter with spatula to flatten slightly. Sauté fritters until cooked through and golden brown, approximately 4 minutes per side. Repeat to make the next 6 fritters. Sprinkle with sea salt and serve with hot sauce.

Crab "Pounds"...

When growing up in Central Florida it was a warm-weather tradition to have crab "pounds" at my grandparents cabin on Lake George, situated in the middle of the Ocala National Forest. Typically, blue crabs are steamed whole, but my grandmother would use seasoned cornmeal to coat the cleaned bodies of the blue crabs and fry them in her cast iron skillet. She'd cover the crab claws with yellow mustard, sprinkle them with seasoning, add a splash of vinegar to the water, and steam the claws to perfection. Much like a low country boil, we'd spread newspaper out on tables, mound the crabs in the center, and armed with our mallets, crackers and picks, we would smash, crack, pick and eat blue crab until we couldn't eat another bite... way before the days of wet wipes, we would be up to our elbows in "mess" with our tongues and fingers stinging from the mustard, vinegar, salt and pepper, and happy as little pigs in mud! So I guess it was no big surprise that Ed and I decided to have a crab pound for our rehearsal dinner. It was such a fun party because so many people had never pounded crab before.

–Susie

Potato Salad with Goat Cheese & Capers

Serves 10 - 12

Florida folklore credits Louis M. Pappamichalopoulos {original owner and founder of famed Florida Pappas Restaurants, originally opened in 1925 in Tarpon Springs} with the addition of hearty potato salad to traditional Greek salad. The story goes that "Pappas" served as an army chef in France during WWI, tucking a bit of potato salad among the lettuce of his Greek salads to help sustain the troops. Regardless of from where this tasty tradition hails... we are grateful for it!   –Susie

3½ - 4 pounds	Yukon Gold potatoes, washed
3 tablespoons	salt, divided
¼ cup	white wine vinegar or other vinegar

Dressing:

⅓ cup	mayonnaise
⅓ cup	sour cream or plain yogurt
3 ounces	soft goat cheese (optional)
1½ teaspoons	Dijon mustard
2 tablespoons	fresh lemon juice
½ teaspoon	black pepper
2	garlic cloves, minced
¼ cup	capers, drained
⅓ cup	fresh-flat leaf parsley or other fresh herbs, chopped
4	green onions, white & light green parts, chopped
	Salt & pepper, to taste

Place potatoes in large stock pot and cover potatoes with water. Over high heat, bring potatoes to a boil, and add 2 tablespoons of salt. Reduce heat to simmer and cook potatoes for 25 minutes, or until tender when pierced with a knife. Meanwhile, in a small dish, dissolve 2 teaspoons salt into vinegar and set aside. Drain potatoes and allow to cool. When cool enough to handle, peel potatoes, and cut into nice size chunks. Spread potato pieces on cookie sheet and pour the vinegar mixture over potatoes. Set aside until cooled to room temperature.

Greek Trim...

This Potato Salad is perfect to serve as part of a Greek salad, especially when feeding a large crowd. Serve with crisp romaine or iceberg lettuce. Arrange salad toppings in rows alongside to make a pretty presentation and guests will have fun creating a custom salad.

Toppings:
Choose your favorites...
- beets
- cucumbers
- blanched green beans
- green onions
- green bell peppers
- red onion slices
- red bell peppers
- tomato wedges
- lemon wedges
- boiled eggs
- chunks of feta cheese
- pepperoncini peppers
- olives
- anchovies
- avocados

... be sure to sprinkle the salad with a little red wine vinegar, olive oil and some dried oregano for a finishing touch.

In medium bowl, mix mayonnaise, sour cream, goat cheese, mustard, lemon juice, 1 teaspoon salt and ½ teaspoon pepper. Place potatoes in large salad bowl, gently lift and fold enough mayo dressing into salad until moistened. Try not to mash potatoes. Carefully add garlic, capers, parsley, and green onions. Taste and add more dressing if needed. Season to taste with salt and pepper. Serve or refrigerate.

Note: To incorporate Pappas' famed flavors as we have here, arrange traditional Greek trim on your salad platter.

Head-on Shrimp

Serves 6-10

The truth is, I have tried many different recipes for head-on shrimp, but I still like this one the best. All of the ingredients can be picked up on the way to the beach. The large amount of pepper makes this dish unique and the butter makes it outstanding. So be heavy handed and use at least one ounce {or more} of pepper and cover each layer of shrimp well. Good crusty bread is mandatory to sop up all the buttery sauce. Dig in, have fun and be happy!   –Susie

3-5 pounds	fresh head-on shrimp, large or jumbo
1	large onion, sliced
24 tablespoons	(3 sticks) butter, cut in tablespoon pieces
1	(2 ounce) can pure ground black pepper
1	(16 ounce) bottle zesty Italian dressing
3	lemons, halved

Preheat oven to 350 degrees.

In a large Dutch oven or heavy-duty roasting pan, create three layers using shrimp, onion, butter, and at least half the can of pepper. Pour Italian dressing over shrimp, and place lemon halves on top. Cover Dutch oven with lid or pan with foil, and bake for 20 minutes. Open oven door, uncover and use a large spoon to carefully redistribute the shrimp and check for doneness. When done, the shrimp should look opaque and start to pull away from the pink shell. *Do not overcook.*

The shrimp may need an additional 10 minutes in the oven, or move them to the stovetop and finish cooking over medium heat, stirring occasionally. *Do not overcook.*

Pour shrimp and sauce onto a large serving platter, and squeeze with roasted lemon halves.

Grab a big glass of wine and serve with warm crusty bread... and plenty of napkins!

Heads Up

Head-on shrimp is key to the success of this recipe because of the fat and richness that the heads add to the sauce.

Catch of the day...

My good friends, Van & Betsy Champion, graciously hosted our family at the coast countless times before we bought our own piece of paradise. Betsy has shoreside dining down to an art, but we do frequently share laughter over meals that almost didn't happen...

In Betsy's Words...
A few years back, we planned a coastal low country boil on Easter for our entire extended family. My husband's only assigned task was to purchase the shrimp {a key component} for the big feast. I had everything else ready to go: potatoes, peppers, sausage, corn, lemons, Old Bay seasoning and had

prepared a table lined with newspaper from which to serve. The only problem - Van got to visiting with friends at the marina and neglected to pick up the shrimp before the seafood shop closed. Needless to say, it made my blood boil. There I was, busting my tail to host a crowd at our beach home for a "casual" low country boil, without shrimp!

Fortunately, my neighbor, Katrice, saw what a pickle I was in and thinking quickly on her feet, presented a creative solution. She directed me to "put on my lipstick," as we were going to get in the boat and plead with the shrimpers anchored out in the bay for some of their catch. It was my only hope. To

make the story even more entertaining, we only had $20 cash between us, so we took some beer with us to sweeten the deal. Picture us, two women, in our 15-foot Whaler, circling a shrimp boat, hollering to capture their attention. The shrimpers had been asleep, but finally emerged and were quite surprised to see us! In the end, we convinced them to give us 6 pounds of shrimp for $20 and two six-packs of PBR. I have no doubt the lipstick helped! I forgave Van for his blunder as he popped the heads off all of the shrimp, and despite the drama, we feasted on some of the freshest shrimp ever.

— Betsy

245

Peach Cobbler

Serves 10-12

When I was young our house was set in the middle of orange groves, but on one side there was an experimental peach orchard. In Florida... crazy! There were many varieties, but my favorite were the white peaches with the bright pink centers. They made me happy because they were the prettiest. If we didn't use peaches, we would sometimes use blueberries or blackberries. Be sure to serve with some good vanilla ice cream. Whipped cream is also good!

–Susie

2 cups	fresh peaches (approx. 4 peaches), peeled & sliced
1 tablespoon	sugar
16 tablespoons	(2 sticks) butter
2 cups	sugar
2 cups	self-rising flour, sifted
2 cups	white wine
	Vanilla ice cream or whipped cream, to serve

Preheat oven to 350 degrees and arrange oven rack to middle position.

In a small bowl, toss peaches with 1 tablespoon of sugar and set aside.

Place butter in a 9 x 13-inch baking dish, and put dish in oven until butter has melted. In a large bowl, whisk sugar, flour, and wine until smooth. Remove dish from oven and pour batter over the butter; *Do not stir.* Using fingers or slotted spoon, drop the sweetened fruit over the batter. Discard extra juice.

Return baking dish to oven and bake for 40-45 minutes or until the center is set and the cobbler is bubbly and golden.

Note: Feel free to use milk as a substitute for the white wine.

From the Curious Cook... Berry Delicious!

I have fond memories of blueberry picking with Slaton and Kate... all of the little ones dressed in their colorful rain boots, carrying tiny beach pails or orange buckets as big as they were, and stuffing more blueberries in their mouths than in the pails. After a few snake scares, tired and sweaty children were glad to eat cobbler with whipped cream and drink cold lemonade while sitting in the backs of trucks and on tailgates. I remember the toothy smiles and sparkly eyes of happy kids!

–Susie

This tasty Peach Cobbler is a favorite of Susie's sweet daughter, Kate.

Here's to finding a little happy...
in Everything!

cheers!

Thank You!

It goes without saying that many, many people shared their time and talents in inspiring the content of this Cookbook. There are so many people to thank, and some we are sure we will miss including by name, but our gratitude is endless.

From The CLEVER Designer...

First and foremost, to Susie, who graciously joined my "pressure-cooking" world to be a part of this adventure. Susie, there are simply not enough words to adequately thank you for sharing so much of yourself within these pages. I'm sure neither of us had any idea we would be here today when we met so many years ago. I could not have asked for a better friend, or a better cook, to have been a part of this incredible experience. To your husband, Ed, and your sweet children, Slaton and Kate, thank you for letting us steal your mom's talents to share with the world in this Cookbook. Count your blessings to have her in your life - you are the lucky ones that get to enjoy her fabulous meals regularly!

To my own family - Mom, Dad, Marcie and Jay - you guys have been on this journey since the very beginning... you truly shaped me into the person I am today. Thank you for your constant presence and encouragement in ALL that I do as well as the many hours of hard work you have {and continue} to give. I know I couldn't have done it without you. Milton, how could I ever thank you enough? I feel your unabiding love and quiet reassurance every single day. Thank you for showing me what a virtue patience can be! And above all, thank you for sharing in the greatest of our life adventure, parenting our three daughters. Kyle, Sara Kate and Mary Parker - the happiness I have in sharing each of your successes is indescribable. Keep reaching for the stars and achieving great things... we are so proud of all that you have - and will - accomplish in life! I love you. Courtney, Taylor and Logan - you three are like my own daughters. I will never forget all of the many great adventures we have had together and sharing in the joy of watching you grow up. Thank you for your love and enthusiasm for Coton Colors.

And, to our customers, who inspire us every day to be bigger and better than the day before. Here's to finding all the Happy we can share!

Bud... "The Optimist!"

Oh Dad, where do I begin? I will never forget the times we spent together in the early days of the business, you scraping pottery, sweeping floors, loading kilns, whatever it took to get the orders out the door. I have loved sharing an office with you from the beginning, when we could look across our desks for quick meetings, the pottery dust swirling between us. It has been a long but oh, so fast road. Your stories have made me laugh more than anything ever has. Thank you for always keeping my feet on the ground and my eyes on the true prize. Although it doesn't always seem like it, I do listen. Your words of encouragement, your guidance, your calm, and intelligence... I couldn't have done it without you. Please know that when all is said and done, the thing that means the most is your *'atta girl!'*. Thank you and I love you.

From The CURIOUS Cook...

First, I must thank God because there have been many moments while working on this project that I have prayed for guidance and strength... but mostly courage, "Oh Lord, I am overwhelmed and if I get through this intact....I promise I will give you credit!" So undeniably and in all seriousness a "thank you, God" is in order.

A huge thank you to Laura who was determined to get me back in the work force after over 10 years removed and because she "hand picked" me to pursue her vision, I will forever be grateful to be a part of this Happy Everything Cookbook project. I have never seen people more motivated or focused as this group. One Coton Colors employee told me when I was commenting on how hard everyone works, "yes, but it doesn't seem hard because Laura always outworks us all." And that is the truth. Coton Colors is a successful company because she is a natural leader {smart, focused, provides direction and motivation}, giving talented people a lot of creative freedom and the final product is ultimately something that we all are proud to be a part of.

Cinque Terre, Italy

I have to credit my grandparents, my parents - Mike and Linda - and my brother Michael. The impact that my family had upon my development as a cook is astounding, not to mention they created childhood memories for me that are as near to perfect as possible.

I would like to thank Ed, my husband, {the word tolerant comes to mind} who has always been my biggest fan. Seeing me through his eyes is always better than how I see myself - always encouraging, rarely critical, and my most trusted friend. I know I married the right guy, and I know that I am better person for it. We have had a lot of fun so far and I'm looking forward to traveling to new places... if we ever get the book to print!

Last, but certainly not least, my smart and funny kids, Slaton and Kate, who give me balance because I have never experienced such joy or anxiety until I became a mom... they are still and will always be my greatest accomplishment!

-Susie

The Team Behind the Scenes...

The walls of the Coton Colors design center hold a enviable amount of talent. Every single one of our employees bring their hardworking energy and enthusiastic spirit to work daily, inspiring one another to give our absolute best and in turn bringing much happiness to our customers. I'm so incredibly proud that this project has been developed completely in-house; from the food styling and recipe development to the photography and story crafting, every member of this amazing team has shared his or her own passion for perfection in this project. Everyone here at Coton Colors has contributed in some way to The Happy Everything Cookbook, but without the tireless efforts of these three people, the Cookbook simply would not exist.

Linley Paske, *Photographer and Marketing Manager*

Like so many of our team members, Linley's talents are multi-faceted, as she is a true marketing guru with a signature specialty behind the lens. She marries these talents beautifully within the pages of the Cookbook, capturing every single photograph with finesse. I love working with someone as passionate as I am... Linley got goose bumps with excitement many, many times as she snapped away, photographing each piece of food and each friend with the same amount of enthusiasm. Thank you, Linley, for portraying us all in the absolute best light possible!

Amanda Koss, *Graphic Designer*

Does "birthing" a cookbook take the same amount of time as becoming a first-time mom? Amanda has tested this in the last nine months. She announced her pregnancy in the same week we began our culinary adventure, and her little belly grew bigger and bigger with her firstborn as we laid out each of the chapters. Fortunately, we managed to not cause early labor in the final days of putting the Cookbook to bed, and it is off to press in the very weeks before her son arrives. Amanda's talented eye has created the most beautiful of layouts for each of our events, showcasing the recipes, photographs and stories perfectly. Thank you, Amanda, for sharing all the happy celebrations of your life with us!

Paige Benton, *Art Manager and Stylist*

A member of our team since the early days {she was hand-painting pottery in our first studio during college in the late 90s!}, Paige possesses an unmatched, polished style. Her artistic eye for sophisticated design and her creative concepts are displayed throughout each page of this book - and in many of the Coton Colors product lines. After so many years together, Paige has become like a member of my family, with a quiet patience that perfectly balances the fast-paced, crazy energy of Coton Colors. Thank you, Paige, for all of your calm contributions.

To our hard-working {even after hundreds of proofs and edits}, in-house editing team, your attention-to-detail and individual contributions shine through in every page!

Kaylan Harrington, Eric Nelson, Jodi Mork, Meghan Melton, Sabrina Pipkin

Many thanks to our storyteller, Nancy Click. The term "jumping in with two feet" perfectly describes Nancy's willingness to contribute to this project. With her quick wit & constant encouragement, she immediately adapted to our Coton Colors {life}style & became an integral member of our team. Her writing talents & creative perspective truly added a unique angle to each & every story, and I am so very grateful that she joined us for this adventure.

To our hard-working, extremely talented artists and illustrators. Your creative talent has helped to bring each page to life.

Kyle Johnson, Lisa Schranz, Corin Schall, Meryl K Walker

And... most especially, these people that have been such a large part of this company. Your heart and soul continue to show through each and everything we accomplish. Thank you for all of the many sacrifices you have made, the hundreds of hours you have given and the plain 'ole hard work and strong determination you continue to provide.

Brian Bachman, Paige Benton, John Blank, Kristin Hendrix, Amanda Koss, Meghan Melton, Eric Nelson, Marcie Parks, Linley Paske, Ashley Trafton

Kristin... thank you! Thanks for always, always, always loving our products {even more than we do!}. You are the spark this company {and I} depend on each and every day. Your good humor, your devotion, your fabulous ideas and your spunk are much enjoyed and very appreciated. Thanks also go to your patient family, Skip, Lyndee and Londyn, for supporting you and in turn, Coton Colors. You are always the winner, whether its a dance contest or a sales contest and in my eyes you will always be a star! Alright, I give... you are not "crazy in the head" and you really do design the perfect napkin.

Acknowledgements

All of these faithful Coton Colors staff members have or will contribute to the success of this new adventure... Marshall Barber, John Blank, Dee Blank, Tisha Brand, Wayne Desilets, Kelly DiMinno, Barrett Frascona, Debbie Hoffman, Mary Parker Johnson, Sara Kate Johnson, Ashley Laing, Taylor Moore, Michael Nolan, Logan Parks, Taylor Parks, Tracy Reavis, Kelly Schmid, Matt Spinks, Kristine Tobi, Lisa Whitlock, Charis Woodall

To our special family who helped us along this journey achieve so much. Thank you for your constant support. We are so lucky to have you in our lives.

Dee & John Blank
Ron, Marcie, Courtney, Taylor & Logan Parks
Jay Blank
Marilyn Johnson
Carol McKee

Brie, Adam, Carson, Emerson & Sutton Hertz
Gail & Kit Moffatt
Josh Suber
Boo, Stephanie & Swayze Suber
Bobbie & Ed Murray, Sr.

Linda & Mike Rou
Mike, Mel, Michael & Josh Rou
Matt, Lindsey, Lilly & JR Thompson

Marcie... thank you! From sharing a room together in the early days to sharing hotel rooms together now, my most favorite thing is our talks, or rather me talking and you listening. You are the one I need to call when I wake up and the one that I just have to call on my way home... to talk some more! Your wise counsel always turns out to be the right thing to do. Thank you for your unwavering and constant support and your never-ending hard work. Although you have always been content to allow me to shine, I know that I couldn't without you. And, darn it... your cooking is always, always better!

To all of those whose smiling faces appear within these pages, and to all of those that volunteered their homes or businesses for photo shoots; allowed us to "gently use" their belongings for props; assisted in photo shoots; contributed recipes; graciously tested recipes and shared their stories:

Catherine Agro
Kathryn Ballard
Patty Barkas
Stan & Tenley Barnes
Jean Bates
Cathy Benton
Dale & Beth Benton
Dick & Hazel Benton
Rick Benton
Wade & Maclain Benton
Sid & Bethany Bowden
Van, Betsy, Handley & Caroline Champion
'Chef' Paul
Vickie Childers
Caroline Conway
Helen Corrigan
Pam Coston
Cuneo Creative Consultants
Mark & Amber Daughtry

Graham Demont
Nicky, Hayley & Tommy DiMinno
Kaley Drawdy
Florida State University Athletic Department
Jenna Fluehr
Jeani Goodwin
Bill & Julz Graham
Ed Greer
Jenna Hall
Emily Hards
Lindsay Harrington
Ronnie & Kim Harrington
Bonnie Hazleton
Skip, Kristin, Lyndee & Londyn Hendrix
Carlana Hoffman
Stephanie Hunter
Liz Jennewein
Pam Jordan
Kathleen Kelly
Ashley Kemp

Paula Kendrick
Sally Lane
Ali Lange
Jeremy & Jessica Little
Marie Long
Eric Marshall
Duncan Martineau
Brittney Mayfield
The Mayfield Group
Lyle McAlister
Susan McAlister
Ann Bannerman McFarlain
Patrick McKee
Lynn, Kiff & Haley Mendoza
DeWitt and Kathy Miller
Serena Moyle
Sandra Myddleton
Eric & Shawna Nelson
Chuck and Amy Newell
Stephanie Olan
David, Linley, Peyton & Palmer Paske
Laura and Will Patrick

Ginger Proctor
Randi Buchanan & Co.
Kaye Robertson
Rosemary Robertson
Jodi, Sophia & Jake Ryon
Robin Safley
Paige Shiver
Six Toms Farm
Andrew Smith
Warren Smith
Delaney Spradley
Rene Stowers
Mark Suber
Austin Leigh Taylor
Mark, Ashley, Mark, Jack & William Trafton
Nicole Trafton
Joni Wallace
Keith Walker
Rick & Michelle Weathersby
Bob Williamson
Justin Wilson

Thank you for sharing your smiles and stories!

- Laura & Susie

To the beloved "furry" family and friends who helped liven up each photo shoot and who continue to bring the biggest smiles to everyone's faces when we browse these pages.

Jazz, Piper, Posy, Tucker, Chica, Charlie, Briggs, Walter, Macy, Gander

Posy enjoyed your company at every photo shoot!

Index

ROUX

1 bell pepper
2 stalks celery

1 1/2 cup oil (not olive oil)
1 2 cups flour (not self-rising)
1 large onion.

note: shrimp will add liquid to gumbo.

add onion, pepper, celery, stir + cover pot.

* hot water to roux after adding

   A heavy pot is a must for making a successful roux. Be sure oil is hot before adding flour. Constant stirring is also a must. Don't answer the door if there is a knock and don't answer the phone if there is a ring. You should have onions, celery and bell pepper already chopped and handy to stop the cooking process at the crucial moment. About half way through the process, the roux will become more liquid, but it will thicken to paste consistency again as it is nearing completion. It is very easy to burn a roux. When the roux reaches the desired color, a rich brown for gumbos (like a Hershey's bar) and a golden brown (like caramel) for sauce piquantes; add the chopped onions, celery and bell pepper to stop the browning process. Continue to stir and remove the pot from the fire. The heat of the roux cooks the onion, celery and bell pepper. * At this point you are ready to proceed with whatever recipe has called for a roux. Unused roux can be stored in the refrigerator for a few days.

add okra, fresh or frozen, cover + lower heat to simmer
seasonings, clean + peel shrimp, add
shrimp 20 min. after above has been simmering
crab meat goes in right before serving. Try not to
stir too much so you have nice lumps of crab.

Mère's original family
Seafood Gumbo Recipe

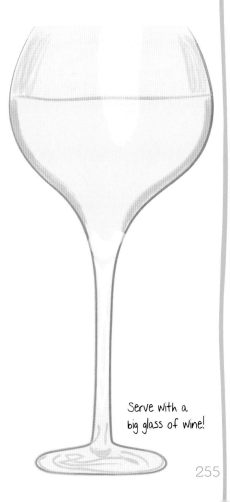

Serve with a
big glass of wine!

Resources

Thank you to the following businesses who were wonderful resources for us in the creation of this book. We encourage you to shop with them as they offer high quality products and friendly service.

Black Fig
1400 Village Square Boulevard, #7
Tallahassee, Florida 32312
850-727-0016
www.blackfig.net

Bradley's Country Store
10655 Centerville Road
Tallahassee, Florida 32309
850-893-1647
www.bradleyscountrystore.com

Coton Colors – Tallahassee
1355 Market St # A9
Tallahassee, FL 32312
850-668-0149
www.coton-colors.com

Coton Colors – Tampa
1300 South Dale Mabry Highway
Tampa, FL 33629-5011
813-254-1251
www.coton-colors.com

Lucy & Leo's Cupcakery
1123 Thomasville Road
Tallahassee, Florida 32303
850-765-0374
www.lucyandleoscupcakery.com

Mineral Springs Seafood & Bait
1612 Coastal Highway
Crawfordville, Florida 32327
850-984-2248

Sweet Grass Dairy
19635 US Highway 19 North
Thomasville, Georgia 31792
229-227-0752
www.sweetgrassdairy.com

Sweet Grass Dairy Cheese Shop
106 North Broad Street
Thomasville, Georgia 31792
229-227-6704

Tallahassee Nurseries
2911 Thomasville Road
Tallahassee, Florida 32308
850-385-2162
www.tallahasseenurseries.com

Tomato Land
1847 Thomasville Road
Tallahassee, Florida 32303
850-425-8416
www.tomatolandtallahassee.com

For information on other items referenced in the cookbook, please check our website:
www.coton-colors.com